Becoming Dynamic

7 Compelling Strategies for Success

Thrive in Greatness!
Elma Hairston

Becoming Dynamic

7 Compelling Strategies for Success

Elma Hairston

Founder and Managing Director
Dynamic Images International LLC

PRESS

Becoming Dynamic: 7 Compelling Strategies for Success
by Elma Hairston

ISBN: 978-0-9972810-1-9
Library of Congress Catalog Card Number: 2016918945

Cover and Book Design: Nick Zelinger
Graphic Design: Maggie Davis
Editor: Cornelia Barr
Photography: Vern Howard
Contributor: Tony Ross

Published by

PRESS

First Edition

Printed in the United States of America

Contents

To Tony, my friend, my coach, without whom I would have continued searching for the key to unlock the door to the potential that lives within.

To my late mother and father, upon whom I bestow an honorary doctorate in parenting.

To my sister Lucille, who has been a mother and disciplinarian. To my brother Billy George, who informed me that my presence and counsel renewed his confidence after a significant loss.

And to my sister Maggie, who brings laughter to all she meets and whose skill and expertise bring to life the graphics you will experience as you progress through your journey to becoming dynamic.

Foreword

BLOOD, SWEAT, AND TEARS! Time and experience! Pride and enthusiasm! Patience and virtue! Authenticity and courage! I believe these are the fundamental characteristics, values, and badges that proven leaders both earn and carry. It is these principles rather than their titles, economic condition, and/or community standing that qualify these people to mentor, inspire, and serve as role models for success. Interestingly, these same characteristics, values, and badges ensure that successful people acquire great titles, economic prosperity, and community influence. The leaders whose lived experiences have afforded them luxury to achieve success are individuals who I believe have a responsibility to share their wisdom. The words on the following pages are the realization of this commitment from one such leader.

In coining the phrase "becoming dynamic," Elma has not only made success and leadership sound provocative, she has effectively created principles that all leaders, especially emerging ones, should follow. The greatest feats in the world, magnificent skyscrapers, and vibrant cities all have blueprints that lead to the desired outcome. Why should it be any different for success? Contrary to the belief of many; success is more than luck; leadership is not simply innate. The two are achieved through time, pressure, methodical calculation, and planning. *Becoming Dynamic* is the blueprint that capitalizes on these things and delivers success and self-actualization.

As the President and CEO of the Urban Leadership Foundation of Colorado, the 2016 Colorado 9 News Leader of the Year, and leader of multiple organizations in my own leadership and success journey, I have seen leaders come and go, themes trend, and fads rise and fall. What I have enjoyed seeing most is the consistent development of leaders, the goals accomplished, the paradigm shifts experienced, and the grit of the individuals associated with the seven principles of this book. There is something almost intoxicating about seeing seeds sown into others by authentic, transparent, and competent leaders.

I suggest you read on but *only* if you understand the jewels that follow are for individuals ready to activate their potential and embrace the success that has always been there for the taking. "Become dynamic." Your achievement waits ahead, so don't look back; besides, why settle for being good when you can be dynamic!

Dr. Ryan E. Ross
President and CEO
Urban Leadership Foundation of Colorado

Acknowledgments

THIS BOOK HAS TAKEN an inordinate amount of work and planning to come together. I am deeply thankful to all the people whose dreams came to fruition because of my counsel and direction. Deferring my dreams in providing counsel and direction to others helped me understand my purpose and set me on a course of reaching my potential and navigating the journey through this book to help you and all who seek higher levels of achievement and success.

Introduction

ALL LIFE'S ENCOUNTERS HAPPEN at an a appropriate moment in time. This encounter with you is happening at a time in my life where experience and time intersect, which equal life maturity. *Life maturity* and *business acumen* are the driving forces that give rise to the authenticity of greatness.

This book has been twenty-five years in the making. Twenty-five years of my experience as a senior executive sales professional at Johnson & Johnson. Twenty-five years of relentless drive, determination and tenacity to internalize what it takes to substantiate that becoming dynamic is a necessary part of success. Twenty-five years of modeling, mentoring, teaching, and guiding others to a path of maximizing their potential. My intent, as you read the book, is to show that one can emerge from a diamond in the rough to a jewel radiating with clarity and definition.

Becoming dynamic is a process I have refined over my career. *Dynamic* is a term that is loosely used to describe the outstanding persona of an individual, place or thing. It is an energetic word that motivates you to envision extraordinary talent. This book will challenge you to embellish my concept of becoming dynamic, expand your comprehension of what is meant by dynamic, and consider dynamic as the guiding principle for your success. Upon completion of this book you have in your hands, *Becoming Dynamic*, you will understand the essence of the intellectual property I have developed and shared here, and the indispensable quality that "becoming dynamic" brings to help you reach the pinnacle of your success.

For over thirty years, I have admired many whose professional presentation and accomplishments can only be characterized as dynamic. They are not only well liked and respected, they are driven by empowering others in their circle of influence. Dynamic people possess *proven values* like integrity, character, work ethic, perseverance, honesty, and a positive attitude. Dynamic people maximize their business presentation by not only being impeccably dressed, but possessing great communication skills, verbal and nonverbal, proper etiquette and manners, and appropriate actions for the occasion. A dynamic individual is poised and ready to communicate his or her mission statement, whether business or personal, and has a plan centered on forging relationships that will help them reach the pinnacle of success in life and career.

This book is a personal journey of communicating what it means to become dynamic in your quest for success. You will experience success by eliminating choices and behaviors that defer your success. It is a book for those who seek the ultimate satisfaction in rising above mediocrity and moving toward greatness in their fullest potential.

You are currently accomplished in many aspects of your life. The skill you acquire from this book is to simply refine your person. It will differentiate you from those in your circle of influence, both professional and personal. It is in differentiating yourself that becoming dynamic emerges.

In becoming dynamic, you will experience a paradigm shift from subconscious competence to conscious competence. Becoming dynamic is strategically planned and deliberately executed. It is a concept that takes deliberate, conscious effort that effectively positions you for success in every aspect of your being. In this concept you want to be mindful that people are subconsciously internalizing your every action. The reaction occurs when an individual begins to make a conscious decision about your ability, your professional image and your actions. It is up to you to leave a positive impression so that in your absence those positive cues are brought to the conscious mind of the individual in position or power to make a favorable decision on your part and in your favor. This process is called *engineering a positive response.* This concept is key to understanding the impact of becoming dynamic.

———

Each of the seven chapters of this book is related to one of the strategies referred to in the title. They have been developed to engineer a positive response that represents a defining moment in your life and career. Strengthening your brand is central to this process.

Chapter 1, *Defining Your Brand: Your Impact is Presence in Motion* is reflective of the impact you make in the image you present, which can determine how successful you become. It is your presence that makes a statement about you. Your impact is presence in motion. Together, making an impact and becoming dynamic form the catalyst for a strong professional brand.

Chapter 2, *Embodying Excellence: Remaining True to Your Dynamic Standard* can create opportunities that may otherwise escape you. Excellence is the premise on which the pinnacle of your success rests. In your pursuit of excellence, it is important to develop a critical eye for detail. As you seek excellence in all you do, procrastination and making excuses as to why a task cannot be achieved has no place in the scheme of things. Always do the right thing, do the task right the first time, and do not accept an explanation that is not based in logic.

Chapter 3, *Leading with Substance, Savvy and Style™: Dynamic Dressing Inspires Success* sets out key basics to follow in order to reach the fullest scope of leadership. Substance inspires confidence by reflecting values from the inside out, from how your character is expressed to how you incorporate guiding principles in the conduct of business. Savvy is executing kindness and consideration in the business or social setting through etiquette. Both in a business and social setting, etiquette is more than the correct knife, spoon and fork; it is the fusion of all the elements that make up the refined individual. Style is creating a look that is appropriate for your industry. It is dressing for the position you seek. Effectively leveraging substance, savvy and style in leadership motivates others to follow. The concept of substance, savvy and style allows you to earn the respect of those that you lead. Earning respect is the recipe for success in your pursuits.

In Chapter 4, *Building Strategic Relationships: Consistency Drives the Dynamics of Confidence,* we emphasize that it is trust that motivates people to take action in your favor and on your behalf. The full potential of success is attained through business relationships built on trust, which ignites confidence. Before you gain the trust and confidence of your customer to act on your product or service, your customer must first gain confidence and trust in you. Only then are you able to move the process along the buying cycle to achieve success in your efforts. Trust is earned by many of the strategies as you proceed through becoming dynamic. The content provides the road map that navigates this course.

Chapter 5, *Finessing Your Success: Leverage your Dynamic Strengths for Growth,* is about pushing through barriers and setbacks. It is the extra effort and attention you give to managing the focus, vision and determination to become successful. Success may be preceded by equivocation, uncertainty and even fear of failure. Dynamic people are driven by their purpose in their mission state-ment and goals set out in their plan of action. Dynamic people become more than a conqueror as they do not allow anything to stand in the way of their dreams.

Chapter 6, *Career Advancement: Preparation Creates Dynamic Opportunities,* will position you for opportunity that ultimately advances your career. Creating opportunity is central to this process. Our goal is to provide the tools to help you reach the pinnacle of your success, find total satisfaction in your life's work and enhance your worth to your employer. In this process, make them want more of you. It is the time invested in education, training and building networks that will bring great benefit in your career advancement endeavor.

Upward mobility in your career can occur as you expand your circle of influence to include people that have the capacity to provide guidance in advancing your career. A mentor and sponsor, not only are key players in strengthening your brand, they are key players in your circle of influence to advance your career.

Chapter 7, *Community Service: Becoming Dynamic by Giving Back* fulfills your desire to serve, builds networks and strengthens your brand. It is giving time, talent and service to your community that makes all that has preceded noteworthy. Community service can help you gain experience in your career objective. It changes lives and is an opportunity for you to share your time and talent to enhance the lives of others. The principles that you will acquire in the chapters of this book should be internalized before you embark on effectively serving your community. The intent is a mutually successful experience.

The sequential chronology of the chapters has been organized so that you can build upon the experiences and principles from each preceding chapter. The book culminates with you allowing me to share the principles that drive my success for the sole purpose of you becoming dynamic. As evidenced by my professional biography located in About the Author, becoming dynamic happened for me, and it can happen for you as you internalize the process and the principles in the book.

When we study sociology, we learn how institutions of society form our worldview. *Becoming Dynamic* encompasses the socialization process that effectively changes the way you see yourself and the impact you make as you interact with others in your career and in your life. The book's goal is to ultimately transform you as a refined person ready to embark upon the things in life and career that you set out to achieve. The value of this project, the book, the workshops and conferences is dependent on the utility you gain from all that is to be experienced, as you embark on your journey to becoming dynamic.

Has your ability been minimized? Has your person been marginalized? Has your fortitude been suppressed? Allow yourself to discover the potential that lives within. The contents of *Becoming Dynamic* is the icing on the cake that many have experienced through the Becoming Dynamic workshops and conferences. Attending these conferences will allow you to dive deeper into the possibilities that await as you explore the refined "you."

The book is the tip of the iceberg in terms of strategies for reaching the pinnacle of success and ultimately becoming dynamic. If you choose to add the excitement and enrichment of the workshops and conferences that await you that will bring to life the reality and relevance of becoming dynamic, you can learn more at www.dynamicimages4you.com.

You have arrived. Your time has come to effectively set yourself on a course that will change your life, for the rest of your life and career.

Now, I understand you have lived in that body of yours for years. You may ask, "Why should I internalize your message now?" My question for you is, "Why not?" Why not embellish the principles of this book to have more, be more and do more in life and career? If nothing more, you will redefine the person you can be for your family, friends and community. You will garner the respect *you* earn by becoming the dynamic and refined person you are meant to be. By internalizing the introduction of this book, you have given yourself permission to read further. Enjoy the ride! The fulfillment of your destiny is near!

Before You Start Assessment Questionnaire

The following assessment will provide direction on becoming dynamic. As you proceed, you will discover answers that will become an integral component of your plan for becoming dynamic. Your answers to these questions will guide you in executing the strategies for becoming dynamic. Take time to deliberate on how the questions apply to your life and career before you proceed.

You may want to use another sheet of paper to provide detailed responses.

Questions:

1. What do you feel are the keys to your success?

   _____

2. What are your strong attributes?

   _____

3. In what areas have you had personal success?

   _____

   Business success?_____

4. What do others recognize as your strengths?

   _____

5. What do people tell you that you do well?

   _____

6. How effective are you in self-managed projects?

    _____

7. What makes you a team player?

    _____

8. What steps are you taking to reach your full potential?

    _____

9. What is the role of table etiquette in your success?

    _____

    Business etiquette?_____

10. Does being around you bring out the best in others?

    _____

    What examples support this fact?_____

11. What steps are you taking to become better at your skill set?

    _____

12. Have you set your goals? Are they written down?

    _____

    Are your goals current? _____

13. How do you manage ethnicity in the workplace?

    _____

14. What do you believe to be your peers' perception of you?

_____

15. What personal relationships hinder your success?

_____

16. What outside activities hinder your success?

_____

17. What is something that you can do right now to advance your career? _____

18. What are your expectations of yourself?

_____

    Your employer? _____

19. How do you feel about your current position?

_____

    Your company? _____

    Your accomplishments in your life, career and community?

_____

_____

_____

1

Defining Your Brand

Your Impact is Presence in Motion

HOW MANY TIMES HAVE you attended a business networking event where you felt that you faded into the shadows of dynamic people whose presence commanded attention? These individuals do not initially utter a word. They have an appealing demeanor. They are impeccably dressed with polished social skills. They are professionals in every sense of the word. These individuals are establishing their brand by their mere presence.

The first compelling strategy in becoming dynamic is defining your brand, and the first step in that process is to strengthen your brand by accentuating the impact of your presence. Your presence should make a statement about you. Your presence allows people to see the dynamic image that lives within. Your impact is "presence in motion." Impact is how you enter a room. Impact is your posture. Impact is the position of your stance. Impact is your knowledge of introductions. Impact is where you position yourself in the room as you network. Impact is understanding how to use your business card. Impact is understanding how to gracefully enter a conversation and exit in order to get the most mileage from the networking or business event. Impact is proper table etiquette. Impact is good manners. If the dynamic person I described above is who you would like to be, then you are in the right place at the right time in your life and career. You are at a place where your greatness can emerge. At the very least, you are now thinking about just how successful you can be by internalizing and executing the strategies in this book.

To gain knowledge on how effective an impact you make in building your brand, fill out the What Is Your Impact? worksheet below. Your responses will make you aware of the impact you make in the image you present.

WHAT IS YOUR IMPACT?

Write in the number 4 for always; three 3 for frequently; two 2 for sometimes; and one 1 for never.

CHECK THE BOX THAT APPLIES:	Always (4 points)	Frequently (3 points)	Sometimes (2 points)	Never (1 point)
Compliments on your appearance				
Compliments from people in power or position				
Choice tables at restaurants				
Preferential treatment from waiters				
People find time to entertain your requests				
You attract positive business relationships				
People go out of their way to please you				
Influential people support your career objective				
You are sought out as a community leader				
Clients have an affinity toward you				
You attract positive personal relationships				
You are promoted in your department or industry				
You effectively manage difficult people				
Others easily make eye contact with you				
Strangers smile at you spontaneously				

Then, add the total of each column horizontally
to determine your impact, as follows:
High: 55-60 Medium: 49-54 Moderate: 43-48 Low: 35-42

This exercise is simply a tool for you to give deliberate thought to your impact in the workplace and in general. It is a useful starting point as you create a strong professional brand.

The impact you make and how successful you will be are interdependent. How far you will go in your career is determined by how dynamic you are. Together, making an impact and becoming dynamic form the catalyst for a strong professional brand. Your brand is built by the impression that others have of you. You want to exemplify those behaviors that drive positive results, thus contributing to the overall great reputation in business you seek.

What comes to your mind when you hear the names Johnson & Johnson, Xerox, Martha Stewart or Oprah Winfrey? Brand recognition. They each have created a strong, recognizable brand based on consistently delivering quality products and services. Look them up and learn more about how they grew successful. Johnson & Johnson is consistently ranked by Fortune magazine as one of the most admired companies in the United States, both for its products and services and for how it treats its employees. Martha Stewart and Oprah both started small; now, as leaders of multi-million dollar media empires, they are household names. The former head of Xerox, Ursula Burns, went from starting as an intern at the company to becoming the first African-American woman to be the CEO of a Fortune 500 company. Their stories show that great success is possible, and that is what you want to achieve.

The importance of the name you represent was constantly reinforced when I was growing up. Each day as I prepared for school, my mother would remind me, "You have a family name to protect. Your actions should not reflect negatively on our family name." The message was that the name "Hairston" has meaning in our community; therefore, protect it. Look, we were a middle-income, blue-collar family, with parents working hard to give their children the best life they could. As matter of fact, by some people's standards, we might have been considered poor. If we were poor, we surely did not know it because of the love, support and proven values that surrounded us. As a result of this attitude, Hairston is a name that has reached prominence in sports, theater, movies, music and literature. It is a name that graces the cover of a best-selling book written by Henry Wiencek titled *The Hairstons: An American Family in Black and White* (1999), an intriguing and interesting read. My ancestors inform me that long before I became an author, that Zora Neale Hurston preceded me. In the old days, "Hairston" was spelled as it sounds, "Hurston." Every family has its folklore, and mine is no exception. At any rate, it is an interesting historical perspective.

Self-Confidence Is Key

Confidence in the way you walk, talk and present yourself is essential in establishing your brand. You bolster your self-confidence when you know that your credibility, consistent work ethic, appearance, performance, character and integrity all strengthen your brand. High moral standards and excellence in all you do differentiate you from those around you, providing yet more ammunition for fueling the strength of your brand. You want to leave a metaphorical "fragrance that lingers after you are gone." In any situation, you want your peers to know you were there; your impact should remain even after you have left a project. By strategically developing your brand as you navigate the corporate power structure, you will be positioned for becoming dynamic.

People Treat You Like You Treat Yourself

People treat you in a manner similar to how you treat yourself. Show respect toward yourself and others will respect you. If you consistently speak positive words about your actions or deeds, people will began to say the same. If you are consistent in your professional presentation, people will began to define you by that presentation. This ultimately strengthens your brand. If you become known for that which is positive and reinforcing, you establish the same mindset in others. Remember your goal is to have people see you in a positive light and carry a positive word about you to others. This is not to imply that you are superficially trying to please everyone you meet. That would be impossible. The goal is to give some deliberate thought to your professional presentation on your journey to strengthening your brand and becoming dynamic.

The Critical Role of Mentors and Sponsors

In your quest to define your brand, the second step in this process is identifying your mentor and sponsor.

Your mentor is a key individual in the company who can help you sharpen your skills and increase your visibility, both in your current area of responsibility and in the company overall. You will want to identify a key individual who is connected in the company and who is willing to share their knowledge and expertise, talking you through the process of gaining knowledge you need to succeed. You may invite this individual for a cup of coffee. Do not be afraid to identify and follow through with him or her. You will be pleasantly surprised at how accommodating most people are. People are generally appreciative of your interest in their career path. Your credibility must be unscathed, of course. You will not be successful gaining assistance in your pursuit of a mentor if you have not done your diligence in strengthening your own brand—specifically being aware of the impact you make. People generally want to be surrounded by successful people, and this relationship is no exception.

Your sponsor is an individual who is in upper management who will use his or her credibility and influence to promote your brand and, ultimately, your career. He or she has clout in the company. You may encounter this individual at a company meeting or networking event. When the opportunity presents itself, introduce yourself and ask if he or she would have a minute for coffee with you. You may encounter a potential sponsor in the elevator. Be prepared with a sixty-second message about your strengths and your goals to motivate the executive to have a brief coffee with you. You want to prepare mentally for this encounter with a strong mission statement that you can communicate with conviction. A point to remember: People are constantly making mental notes as they observe your demeanor, actions and contributions to the team. Be mindful. Be observant of those who have an affinity for you and vice versa. There are individuals whom you can count on to fuel your support system by virtue of the way in which you conduct yourself in the work environment.

Your Professional Image Parallels Your Self-Worth

The third step in defining your brand is your professional image. Your professional image is one that should be appropriate for your industry. It is strategically planned and deliberately executed. It is the cornerstone of positive self-esteem. It parallels self-worth. Your professional image can propel you to success or it can leave you unworthy of a second glance. Image is whom we see. Dynamic is who you are. Dynamic is what people experience when being in your presence. It is like the communication continuum, which is the relationship between the sender and receiver. Your image sends the message and stimulates a dynamic response on the part of the receiver. This response can be subconscious or conscious, positive or negative.

The dress code in many work environments is currently business casual. Whether conservative or business casual, your look should be appropriate for your profession.

Your professional image can enhance your effectiveness in business, community and your personal life. It is more than external appearances. It is your ability to effectively communicate verbally and nonverbally. People are making mental notes about your persona. It is important that those notes are positive. To ensure you stay on track with your quest to become dynamic and strengthen your brand, you must be consistent in your actions, words and deeds. You must use your image to motivate others to follow your lead. Remember, as referenced in the introduction, you want to bring to the conscious mind those attributes that are positive and that can overall enhance your effectiveness and success in all your pursuits.

Communication Is More Than Words

The fourth step in strengthening your brand is effective communication. Your ability to speak clearly, concisely and to the point is critical in this process. You do not want to have a reputation of "talking loudly and communicating little" in the way of meaningful dialogue. Your reputation defines your person and follows you throughout your career. You want your communication to be meaningful, thought provoking and intellectually sound.

I learned to speak well literally at my mother's knee. My mother used to sit me on her lap, with my face in front of hers, and teach me how to speak correctly. She would always speak with me facing her because she wanted me to see how she articulated words so that I would do the same. She would speak to me at my level, never towering over me as she spoke. She seemed to be conscious of her body language, using eye movements and facial expressions as tools to move to the next level of communication, forming words into sentences. Thanks to her, I am able to use language effectively and articulately.

In all written communications, from an office memo or email to a contract or client analysis white paper, review your copy to ensure it is grammatically correct and factually sound. You should also confirm that you are communicating your thoughts completely and effectively. How many times have you completed a statement and you felt that you did not fully communicate your key thoughts? Pay close attention to the tone of your message to be sure it conveys respect and deference. Email is especially challenging—hints of sarcasm, flippancy, or incomplete information can be magnified in the recipient's mind and reflect badly on you and your company.

Oral presentations are where a dynamic image makes an indelible impression. Companies are seeking the best and the brightest, and focusing on the delivery of your message is paramount in becoming dynamic. Joining a speaker's bureau, like Toastmasters International, provides a way to sharpen this skill. A simple way to build an understanding of how you come across in a presentation is to practice in front of a mirror. You may also have a friend video you via your cell phone in order to determine where you need to strengthen your technique. Voice inflection, tone and pitch are all important components of delivery. Learn to modulate the tone of your voice so that you do not speak in a monotone, and vary your intonation to reflect passion or sincerity. You can motivate with the tone of your voice or you can discourage with the tone of your voice. Articulation is important, so be sure you verbalize all syllables in each word you speak. Speak at a pace that is understandable and not too fast. The meaning of your message can get lost if you speak too fast. Most of us encounter a bit of nervousness at the thought of speaking. There is a tendency to speak faster when you are nervous. When you practice your speech, try speaking at a slower than normal pace. At the time of your actual presentation, your pace will pick up slightly, making a strong connection with your audience.

Another area of communication is your social media presence. Your private profile reflects on the public perception of you as a professional. Be sure that, whatever you do on Saturday night, what you post on Facebook is something you would be happy to share with your boss on Monday morning.

Power Words

Language is powerful, and certain words—what I call power words—can speak volumes in their ability to refine your persona. Power words can differentiate you from others in your environment, as you embark on becoming dynamic, power words motivate people to action. Power words not only define the person using them but also motivate the person receiving the communication. Power words can give meaning to your contribution to the company, team or networking opportunity. The worksheet below consists of power words that you can incorporate in your daily application of defining your strengths.

Power Words Worksheet

Which words define you and your strengths? Here are the words I consider key power words. Next to each word, write how you fulfill the aspect of that power word. Start with the power word that you feel best describes your strength and what you bring to your organization.

PRINCIPLED
A Principled Person possesses:
  ➤ integrity and honesty
  ➤ Strong sense of fairness
  ➤ Respect for the dignity of others
  ➤ Sense of responsibility for actions
    and consequences	

DRIVE
A Driven Person shows:
  ➤ Clear direction
  ➤ Vision that separates best from average
  ➤ Can-do spirit; not a procrastinator
  ➤ Sense of competitiveness	

TENACITY
A Tenacious Person:
  ➤ Never gives up
  ➤ Never stops trying
  ➤ Does whatever is required to accomplish a goal
  ➤ Does not complain or find ways not to
    accomplish a goal	

DETERMINATION
A Determined Person remains:
  ➤ Intent on achieving a goal
  ➤ Firm in the belief that nothing is impossible
  ➤ Committed to never letting anyone or anything
    stand in the way of your dreams
  ➤ Understanding your potential	

Power Words Worksheet *continued*

Add your own power words here:	

The Power Words worksheet brings to life phrases you can utilize to answer many of the questions on the Before You Start questionnaire on page 19. The phrases can be applied to provide answers to questions that can clearly define what you "bring to the table" in the full scope of maximizing your ability and the differentiating keys that unlock the door to your full potential.

The Five Ps of Becoming Dynamic

The fifth step in strengthening your brand is what I call the Five Ps: —Passion, Preparation, Practice, Performance and Polish.

Passion is compelling enthusiasm. Passion is the focus that gives meaning or shape to your goals. Passion is the driving force that keeps you focused. Approach your day with anticipation and a positive attitude. Believe that something good is going to happen because of the positive attitude you exemplify. Even if things are not going as well as you like on any given day, your positive prospective will prevail. It may be something as simple as a kind gesture from you or adding a smile to someone's day. As my mother would say, "If you meet someone without a smile, give them one of yours."

The passion you exemplify in your career strengthens your brand in becoming dynamic. Once my co-worker said, "We are glad you are on our team. We would not want to be your competition." My passion to be the best at my profession was revealed in my work ethic, drive and determination to succeed. My tenacity kept me at the top of my game. In serving your clients, you must leave no stone unturned. Prompt follow-up, product knowledge, business acumen and going that extra mile, all support your passion and get the results that drive success.

I once had a client who would not make time to see me despite numerous office calls, which made meeting my sales goals at that time very difficult. The reason he did not make time for me was his past experience with other representatives who were not prepared to answer his probing questions, who failed to present from peer-reviewed articles and whose professional image left much to be desired. In becoming dynamic, using your professional image to strengthen the perception of the standard for your industry is paramount. This is a message those sales representatives ignored. You are not only representing yourself, but you represent your company, your industry and your peers. I called this "paving a positive path for others." It is important that you unselfishly internalize that it is not all about you.

As for my client, I was at a crossroads. I had done everything possible in terms of customer follow-up, providing information about clinical trials, and building rapport with the office staff through educational in-services. After persisting for three months, I was granted a meeting. As I walked into the client's office, he complimented me on my professional attire and demeanor, which I was known for in the industry. Needless to say, my product knowledge, business acumen and passion for my work garnered a high level of respect as well. I not only paved the way for other meetings, I set a precedent. I was one of the few company representatives that the client would allow to set an appointment. When the client needed me to answer questions, I had his direct line to give him the information. This client became one of my best allies and contributed significantly to my success. My brand was strengthened in the industry because of the positive outcome of this experience.

Passion in your efforts will become internalized over time. It will set you apart. When the opportunity presents itself, your clients will remember you and how you differentiated yourself from others. The positive comments this doctor communicated to other colleagues in this success story not only opened the door for additional business, they built my brand with other clients in the industry. Professional demeanor, in-depth expertise, sound product knowledge and impeccable dress contributes significantly to becoming dynamic and provided the turning point for me to capitalize on this experience.

Preparation is the catalyst for excellence in performance. In the business environment of today, far too many people simply aim to accomplish the bare minimum. Dynamic individuals are poised with the tools to soar to the highest levels of achievement. They are not only prepared to create opportunity for themselves but for others, as well.

In my career, I was known as the person who had the project ready before management asked for it. I was always prepared for a presentation long before it was due. This kept me consistently one step ahead of the competition. In the story I just shared, preparation was key for my success. Picture this: I was sitting at the desk of my client. He was asking technical questions, and I was prepared to give acceptable FDA-approved responses that were compliant and fulfilled the need to know. It was difficult and it was stressful, but I kept in mind a mantra from one of our senior managers: "Never let them see you sweat." Being prepared made it possible for me to achieve success.

It is moments like these that build professional prowess. There is satisfaction, as I rest at the end of the day, in knowing my actions were ethical, honest and professional. You should have no regrets about your business dealings. You must know you have done your best and that your level of excellence was second to none. You can leave any business encounter with a clear sense of accomplishment and reassurance of your self-worth. As your standard of excellence is revealed and you sincerely show deference to others, your authenticity emerges and you are on your way to becoming dynamic.

Practice is where the best becomes better. In my twenty years as a senior executive sales professional, I invested thousands of hours perfecting my life's work. I consider this as "time spent becoming dynamic." Take the proverb "practice makes perfect" to heart, because repetition evokes perfection. Practice articulation by rehearsing your presentation in front of a mirror. Record yourself making a presentation. This provides a great critique.

Role-play a real-life situation with a family member or friend. Select five questions from the Before You Start questionnaire on page 19. Prepare thoughtful answers. Then present the answers in the presence of a friend, family member or coworker, allowing them to critique your delivery, your passion and your appeal. This exercise will help you understand the impression you make on your audience and the accuracy and precision you display in your delivery. This very basic experience will prove to be valuable in the future.

As you pursue your career, read about, study, and model yourself on people in your environment who are dynamic. Practice their positive behaviors. Research your product. Educate yourself on company financial trends. Understand the company culture and rank among industry leaders. Understand the causes your company is passionate about and volunteer in those areas. These techniques will amazingly enhance your journey toward becoming dynamic.

Performance is where information and comprehension intersect. Your performance should be executed so well that all who experience you will not forget that you were there. Everything you touch in becoming dynamic should have your brand written all over it. I was once invited to a ceremony where I received recognition at the same time as a prominent political figure. While we stood offstage preparing our lineup, the official said, "I know you had a hand in this event, it's so elegant." Unfortunately, I did not play a role in organizing the program, but because he had experienced others that I coordinated, my brand was uppermost in his mind. Our goal is to use the collective strategies in this book to define your brand and leave a lasting impact in all you do. In the final analysis, the economic and financial impact can be substantial in your quest for becoming dynamic.

Polish is a central characteristic of the refined, dynamic individual. Polish consists of many facets that contribute to your making a dynamic impression. Openness to new ideas plays a role; become familiar with other cultures, stay abreast of current events, understand stock trends and keep abreast of current and compelling books. Be active in your community. Volunteer in activities that define your corporate culture. If you do not know how to play golf, you should learn. Many business opportunities and transactions occur on the golf course. You do not have to become a professional golfer; just learn the basics.

Business etiquette is also essential to the refined businessman or -woman. Understanding the placement and correct use of eating utensils show that you have taken the time to learn this skill. It will prevent embarrassment on your part when entertaining clients or having dinner with company management. How many times have you been at a dinner and it is apparent that no one around the table really knows the correct knife, spoon or fork with which to begin the meal or realizes that the napkin placed on the lap starts the meal? Properly introducing colleagues attending a business networking event or meeting is another way you finesse your business etiquette and demonstrate your polish.

When I would entertain a very important client for lunch, I made sure I arrived at the restaurant in time to take care of all the small details that would make the meal go smoothly. First, I selected an upscale restaurant where I was well known. This was apparent when I walked in the door. I was also known for tipping well and as a result was treated like royalty. I made sure my credit card information was left with the waiter ahead of time. At the completion of the meal, the waiter walked to the table and simply said, "Everything is taken care of, Ms. Hairston." This made an impression and set me apart from my peers. After I walked with my client to the door and said farewell, I returned inside the restaurant to handle the details of the tip for the waiter and close out the transaction. It was apparent that I was willing to go that extra mile to show the client the level of class, style and attention I would bring to every aspect of the account.

Executing the Five Ps brings definition and clarity to the overall philosophy of becoming dynamic. Spend time perfecting your skills and demonstrating your willingness to learn new things, and you will create opportunities to advance in your career.

Your brand, as you have seen in this chapter, is composed of many elements. As you define and refine your brand, your impact will become increasingly dynamic. When you effectively make an impact, you strongly influence outcomes that enhance your success in life, career and business. The following chapters will provide in-depth guidance in mastering the skills you need to achieve this success by becoming dynamic.

2

Embodying Excellence

Remaining True to Your Dynamic Standard

EXCELLENCE AS A STATE of mind is the second strategy in becoming dynamic. Whether you agree with me or not, there is a quality standard and an order to the progression of any process. You achieve excellence by consistently executing this high standard in all you do. Developing a mindset of excellence is no exception. You have already achieved excellence in many aspects of your life and career. We will explore the role that a mindset of excellence—what I call my "E" game—plays in making the difference as you embark upon becoming dynamic.

Excellence is the premise on which the pinnacle of your success rests. But how can excellence be measured? I rely on what I call proven values, time-tested principles that clarify what you need to do to make excellence the defining principle of your brand. We will discuss proven values later in the chapter.

Consistently Embody Excellence

Excellence starts with you. Your image should typify excellence. Because opportunity can be found at almost every turn, it is imperative that you internalize this fact. You will not have a second chance to make a first impression, so always be prepared with a clear sense of your proven values and what you represent in your profession. The impression you make can, in fact, create opportunity in some unexpected places.

You stop by Starbucks to get a cup of coffee and the CEO of a corporation just happens to be waiting in line. You have got your "E" game on. You are dressed for success. You strike up a conversation. You exchange business cards, and the rest is history—you have created a career opportunity.

A team member approaches the meeting dressed impeccably. He circles the conference table handing out his printed reference materials. The handouts do not match his appearance: it is printed on cheap paper, the content is poorly organized, and it contains several typographic errors. He has blown his credibility among his peers. He has let his team members and managers down. For him, becoming dynamic is deferred because he is not executing excellence in every part of his being and in his every action.

Remain at the Top of Your Game

As you strive to become dynamic, be at the top of your game at all times. Always look your best, exercising courtesy and deference in all your actions. Your standard of excellence will affect the environment for your coworkers and all those around you. Go that extra mile to set high standards among your peers. Some people put their best foot forward only in the presence of management or for someone they want to impress. To build a strong brand that will move your career and guarantee the success in your endeavors, recognize that support comes from all around you, and that excellence in every interaction is paramount. Running into a CEO of a company is very real possibility that you can experience on any given day. The first impression is not initially focused on your education, your contacts or your experience. The first impression is based on your "presence in motion," the subconscious competence embodied in your motivation to start a dialogue and the message sent by your professional presentation.

You have a responsibility to your own authenticity to develop excellence as a state of mind. Going above and beyond supports your commitment to excellence. When the team member shared substandard meeting handouts, he lost the trust of his team and will have to work hard to get it back. Once you have lost the trust of others, it is hard to regain. It is not to say that it is impossible, but difficult to gain.

The very first training seminar that I experienced some twenty-five years ago was called "Doing It Right the First Time." The content of the seminar proved to be valuable, and I keep a few key concepts in the archives of my historical reference. Let me share some that have been beneficial to me in my pursuit of excellence and can be beneficial in your pursuit of becoming dynamic.

- ➢ Develop an affinity for detail
- ➢ Do not make excuses as to why a task cannot be achieved
- ➢ Do not procrastinate
- ➢ Do not wait for someone to give you all the details
- ➢ Develop an affinity to dig deeper
- ➢ Do not accept an explanation that is not based in logic
- ➢ Doing the right thing the first time saves time, effort and energy

Never Allow Anyone to Place Their Trash in Your Can

Let's face it—there are some that would have you fail in your quest for success. That human factor exists in all we pursue. As you strive to do your best, there will be people who will place barriers to your success. You must persevere. Do not allow what others say or do to impede your progression to success and ultimately to becoming dynamic. Negative words can have no impact on you unless you internalize them as truth. As my mother would say, "Never allow anyone to place their trash in your can." How you react to what is said to you determines its impact, so develop positive responses for negative dialogue centered in a bold confident stance on your truth.

Your life should be filled with positive and life-sustaining words of empowerment, not words and actions that shame or degrade. Misery loves company. Many people are not in a secure place. They adopt a defeatist posture that prevents them from achieving success. You must make a conscious effort to *choose* to thrive. The substance of your persona begs for this transformation before you can internalize the concept of becoming dynamic. You must make a decision to move past that negative place to a place where you can reach the potential you have inside. You want to seek a place where you can rest in knowing that a mindset of excellence is at the core of your proven values.

If you observe habits in your environment that do not define excellence for you, do not let that alter your sense of excellence. Be mindful about your associations with individuals who do not meet your high standards. Do not engage in dialogue that does not define your standard of excellence. Do not become a party to the old adage, "because everyone else is doing it, it must be okay." It takes your focus off your goals. With this focus, you will be on your way to becoming dynamic.

The Roots of Excellence Start Early in Life

It is my belief that excellence as a state of mind starts with our environment early in life. Our environment has a big impact on our persona and our values. I was fortunate that my parents set the environment for success that empowered me to embrace the essence of excellence.

Does that mean that if your environment did not encourage you to set goals and pursue excellence, you can't succeed? No! The fact that you are reading this book means that you are ready to embrace excellence. The same rules apply: Find a mentor at your workplace or in your social circle, set goals for yourself, and identify proven values that will guide your steps as you strive to embody these principles.

Positive influences in your life are so very important. When I was a girl, my mother and I used to have teatime. My mother, my dolls, and I would be seated at a small table, properly set with my miniature tea set. Through the ritual of teatime, she shared her wisdom on excellence. Excellence must be modeled in the way you walk (head up and shoulders back), the way you speak, and the way you conduct yourself in public and private. My mother used to say "the way in which you conduct yourself at home is an indicator of how you conduct yourself in public." She gave me an example: "Just observe how children act in public, good or bad. It is a direct reflection of how they are allowed to act at home." Order is a learned behavior and is needless to say, learned early in life. My mother also used to say, "If your house is out of order, then your life is out of order." These are the words of wisdom that I can truly say directed my path to becoming dynamic. The precision of the order of the table was a testament to her attention to excellence. This precision was not only exemplified in the miniature tea set place setting but in our every meal. This experience had long-term implications on my life and career.

Another time my mother reserved for sharing her focus on excellence was when she had me sit in a small chair at the end of the ironing board as she ironed my dad's shirts. At the time I wished I were outside with my friends having fun instead of listening to my mother. I am now thankful for those moments, which then seemed endless, as though time stood still. As she ironed each shirt, she meticulously folded and placed it in the drawer with precision. Observing this process taught me to execute with detail and order. This simple process reinforced my worldview of excellence.

My mother had an in-home daycare where she shared the same emphasis on excellence with other children as she did with her own. She understood that children model people around them. She combined high expectations that children would learn to read, speak articulately and develop social skills, with kindness and a supportive environment that built their self-esteem. All the children in her daycare could read before they entered first grade. She used these experiences as teaching moments to ensure perfection in the spoken word and reading. We all benefited mightily from this experience.

Nowadays, the environment in which we find ourselves makes it so easy to give up without experiencing the end result. We are often discouraged by people in our lives whom we value and trust, which can lead many to choose to give up. My mother never made allowances for this mindset. For her and for us, quitting was not an option. We always had to finish what we started. Whenever I pursued any extracurricular activity in school, she would say, "I want you to think about what you are about to embark upon, because quitting is not an option." This stick-to-it state of mind is the fuel for becoming dynamic.

She often reminded me of the story of the tortoise and the hare. You know the story: The tortoise was slow and steady. The hare was swift. He ran circles around the tortoise. The hare wasted time and energy procrastinating and resting on his laurels. Wouldn't you know it, the steady but sure tortoise kept his eye on the prize and finished the race as the winner. By the time the rabbit reached the finish line, the tortoise had already met and exceeded his goal—crossing the finish line with time to spare. Life is like that. Time can slip away so quickly. It is important to capitalize upon and cherish each moment in life. Enjoy your time with friends and family. Do not spend time on negative thoughts and self-defeating actions. Do not waste time envying someone else's gift and talents. Spend that time sharpening your own.

Excellence is crossing the finish line in record time by staying the course, focusing on the end result, and ultimately utilizing the drive, determination and tenacity it takes to succeed.

Excellence Sets You Apart

Excellence is the defining quality that sets you apart from the rest. Do not focus on the gifts of others. Your focus must remain on what you bring to the table. You must know that the talent you have is a blessing and no one can do it better because it is yours. It can only be taken away at your permission. Negative, self-defeating thoughts can impact you only if you allow yourself to internalize them. You must understand that you were placed on this earth to do great things. You deserve to have the best in doing your best. You short-change yourself when you allow someone to steal your joy in this process. When you allow someone or something to steal your joy, you are left feeling defeated. This is a time for you to bring those subconscious cues to mind where your accomplishments outweigh your failures. As you focus on these accomplishments, self-esteem increases and your perspective is enhanced.

Excellence is taking pride in who you are and the work that you do. It is so easy to become complacent because the norm is seemingly doing just enough to meet the average grade. Excellence is doing your job so well that others look to you for guidance. Excellence is dressing in a way so that others want to emulate you. As you build this reputation among your peers, you not only build your self-esteem, you also strengthen your brand. Becoming dynamic is imminent.

You are consistently being compared to others in your environment. I was being compared to the representatives that came before me, which resulted in my not being granted an appointment. As I reflect, it was not that the client was being uncooperative, he based his decision on how representatives who came before me conducted themselves in the business environment. I had to work twice as hard to get in the door as a result, but once I did, my commitment to excellence impressed him and became the basis of a long-lasting business relationship.

Proven Values as a Cornerstone of Excellence

How do proven values drive the essence of excellence? They are time-tested, widely respected standards that you can use to assess your own commitment to excellent performance. They are also values that will be recognized by those around you. The proven values that I find most compelling are integrity, character, work ethic, perseverance, honesty, and positive attitude.

I like to think of proven values as a bridge between commitment to excellence and becoming dynamic. They involve both your work life and your personal life; most importantly, they work together, strengthening each other and becoming a more dynamic part of how you present yourself. After exploring the proven values discussed here, you will have a chance to reflect on how you incorporate these values in your life and explore the impact that proven values have on developing your core of excellence.

Integrity

Your integrity speaks volumes about your persona. It is a firm adherence to a standard or code of conduct. To exhibit integrity, you must "say what you mean, and mean what you say." You must not only "talk the talk," you have to "walk the walk." How many times have you experienced someone who volunteers to perform a task as a committee or team member and does not follow through? I always give team members the opportunity to redeem themselves. Do they not follow through because they did not understand the methods for achieving the task or have they built a reputation of not following through? In the latter case, no one takes you seriously. In the former case, have the fortitude to ask for more direction or clarification so you can complete the task. In your estimation, which behavior would build your integrity and which one would not? Easy answer: ask for clarification. Failure to ask for help delays completion of the task. A reputation of procrastination has no place in your integrity portfolio as you develop a mindset of excellence.

Character

Your character is the moral fiber on which your image is built and excellence can emerge. No one proven value, power word or impact statement stands alone. It is character around which all else revolves. Character, much like image, sets you apart. Good character comprises much of the content on which this book is based. We reflected earlier on how important it is to respect yourself; when you project self-respect, others will respect you. When you take responsibility for your actions and do the task right the first time, you are showing character. In leadership and generally in all human interaction, treating people fairly and decently is of importance in developing character; the roots of etiquette and manners grow from an impulse to interact kindly and with care for one another. Lastly, citizenship is your obligation to adhere to the standards and obligations that are inherently based on doing the right thing and doing right by your fellow man or woman.

Work Ethic

A strong work ethic is so very important to building your brand and enhancing the impact in the image you present. Work ethic is a commitment to the belief that work is morally good. You want to be visible to decision makers in your industry who have the power to positively impact your brand, your income and your upward mobility. There is no pretense here. In my profession, physicians observed me studying clinical trials in the medical library. I would visit my hospital accounts early, when physicians were making rounds. I would spend time studiously reviewing a clinical trial while waiting for my appointment to see a physician, while I observed my colleagues discussing their plans for the weekend. There is a time and place for everything, and discussing plans for the weekend in the presence of patients and others is in poor taste and quite inconsiderate in a business environment. Business etiquette is a must in situations like this. Making the most of your work hours is critical in sharpening your skill in creating a mind-set of excellence.

Perseverance

Perseverance is critical in developing the level of excellence that it takes for becoming dynamic. Commitment to your goal or purpose is mission-critical to your developing a mindset of excellence. Commitment is remaining true to your person and not allowing anyone to stand in the way of your dreams and aspirations. As mentioned previously, people will place barriers in your path. In order to succeed, you must sometimes love those who are the perpetrators from afar. You cannot continually allow individuals or situations to infringe upon the space you have reserved to spread your wings and grow to higher levels of accomplishment. Refer to the Before You Start questionnaire and identify situations, both personal and professional, that prevent you from moving forward. I think most of my associates would say that I am a good friend and a savvy businessperson and possess an indwelling desire to achieve. But I set boundaries and I challenge those in my circle of influence to provide solutions and not simply state the problem. My associates have one opportunity to state the concern. We develop a plan of action. Look to the future with anticipation and do not dwell on the past.

Honesty

Honesty works in concert with many of the previously stated proven values to create a synergistic effect that shapes the mindset of excellence. Honesty is the key that unlocks the door to increased responsibility. Expense accounts are a part of most professionals' armamentarium of client interaction as they conduct business. Lack of discipline can lead to abuse of this privilege. An individual's ability to manage personal finances is a determining factor in the hiring process for some companies and positions where expense accounts are typical. This is directly related to making an honesty call in a person's character to support the trust factor in the hiring process. There is a distinct difference between lack of discipline or an honest mistake. Here is a case in point: Not paying attention to which card I was using, I once pulled out my company card and made a personal purchase on the company card. Mixing the two was outside company policy. Instead of having the transaction credited, I informed management of the inadvertent error, submitted a memo of explanation with the expense report and all was well. If you make a mistake, admit it and move on. We can forgive an admission of a mistake; the problem lies in the cover-up. When your honesty is compromised, your integrity is at risk. Best practice, honesty is the best policy.

Positive Attitude

A minister once told me in a very arcane manner, "What's in you will reveal itself in your attitude." Creating an attitude of excellence is what you seek in the process of becoming dynamic. A positive attitude keeps you looking ahead and anticipating great things. Do not allow anyone to "steal" your attitude by placing negativity in your path. It is a matter of perspective, as mentioned earlier. In your assessment, your perspective can drive your worldview of how you perceive things that are important to you in your environment. It can provide a benchmark in adopting the positive perspective that it takes to get results. Developing a consistent positive attitude takes deliberate thought and focused introspection. One thing is for sure, your attitude can determine how successful you are, how far you succeed and how people interact with you. Your demeanor or temperament can either provide fuel for the flame or extinguish the flame altogether. Develop the habit of saying a kind word or performing a kind gesture to dismantle a potentially bad situation. Amicable outcomes should be the goal.

Now, take the time to reflect on the proven values discussed here. Make a check indicating whether you feel you currently incorporate each value in becoming dynamic, or whether you need to work to incorporate that value. Write in how you feel you project this value in the workplace. These results will help you successfully move forward in your quest for excellence and will ultimately have an impact on your career advancement.

Proven Values Worksheet

		How I project this proven value
Integrity ➤ Adhere to that which is acceptable ➤ A strong sense of right and wrong	☐ Currently possess ☐ Need to incorporate	_____ _____ _____
Character ➤ Standards of conduct ➤ Abiding by rules	☐ Currently possess ☐ Need to incorporate	_____ _____ _____
Work Ethic ➤ Be on time ➤ Call in if absent ➤ Do your task better than anyone ➤ Meet the challenge; push yourself to the limit	☐ Currently possess ☐ Need to incorporate ☐ Currently possess ☐ Need to incorporate	 _____ _____ _____
Perseverance ➤ Never give up ➤ Stay focused on the goal	☐ Currently possess ☐ Need to incorporate	_____ _____ _____
Honesty ➤ Set the standard ➤ Honesty is the best policy	☐ Currently possess ☐ Need to incorporate	_____ _____ _____
Positive Attitude: ➤ Attitude determines altitude ➤ Keeps you looking ahead and achieving goals	☐ Currently possess ☐ Need to incorporate	_____ _____ _____

As you aspire to the highest levels of excellence, your achievements will be the icing on the cake. Achieving through excellence pushes you to the limit to meet any challenges you encounter. When my co-worker stated, "I am glad you are on our team and not the competition," he was acknowledging that my dedication to proven values and my mindset of excellence fueled my achievement. This combination will be your inspiration to do your task better than anyone, to be the best at your life's work.

I challenge you to remember five things in approaching this process: (1) wake up every morning with expectation, (2) listen to your positive inner voice, (3) do not allow negativity to invade your space, (4) remain true to your dynamic standard, and (5) think of a happier time when you feel your world is closing in.

We have focused on excellence thus far because excellence occupies a huge space in the overall scheme of things. It is worth re-emphasizing what excellence is. Excellence is possessing the quality of outstanding performance and setting a high standard. Reflect on your most recent performance review. Can you truly say you performed in an outstanding way? Can you think of ways you can be better at your job specifications? Are you setting an excellent example for your team members to follow? As referenced in chapter 1, are you making the impact you desire? Can people see the dynamic person that you truly are or aspire to be? Recall that my professional demeanor, in-depth product knowledge and professional presentation were the drivers that landed me a meeting with a difficult-to-see client. I challenge you to use these same principles to show that you have the excellence in performance and standard to take you to the next level.

3

Leading with Substance, Savvy and Style™

Dynamic Dressing Inspires Success

SUBSTANCE, SAVVY AND STYLE are three terms that have comprised the core of my approach to leadership for many years. These terms give definition to becoming dynamic. When we add a great leader to the equation, we create a dynamic individual destined for success.

A leader who embodies substance, savvy and style inspires confidence in others and motivates people to follow. *Substance* speaks to substantial quality or character. A leader needs to demonstrate character and respect for others to motivate them to follow. *Savvy* is defined as having the understanding that allows you to navigate business and social situations with grace. Practical understanding of people, projects and position plays a significant role in this process. And *style* is distinctive expression. An individual's attention to style in dress and behavior sets the standard that commands respect and embodies leadership potential.

What Makes a Leader?

Twenty-five years in corporate America shaped my leadership philosophy. It set the premise of the substance needed for effective leadership. The principles of this premise is centered on leaving things in better shape than I found them, empowering people to find their strengths, and inspiring confidence in others. I share with you my

"Pearls of Wisdom," which are the drivers of substantive leadership and contributed to my success in the business world:

- ➢ Your greatest accomplishment is helping others accomplish great things
- ➢ Be prepared to live with the decisions you make
- ➢ Challenge others to be the best they can be
- ➢ Be consistent in your words, actions and deeds
- ➢ Your greatest failure is preventing others from achieving greatness

Treating people decently and helping others become successful is key to the concept of becoming a dynamic leader. This process requires very deliberate thought on your part. A dynamic leader listens with understanding and puts empathy for the other person paramount. He or she knows that bias, stereotype, racism, sexism and any attitude that negatively defines people will interfere with the ability to attentively listen with understanding. A true leader knows that embracing diversity of thought is essential to becoming dynamic. I am discussing individual leaders here, but corporations in their quest for success could take a few notes as well.

Leaders Are Open to Diversity

It is people—individual leaders—who comprise corporations. It stands to reason that the leaders in corporations are in a position to drive the principles of listening and embracing diversity. In my estimation, many a corporation is not as profitable as it could or should be because diversity of thought is lacking in the upper echelons of the company. Diversity is not an end in itself; its value is that it brings fresh perspectives to the table that probably would not arise from a more homogeneous group. Diversity is sometimes marginalized where major decisions are made. When the leaders at the top and throughout the company are of the same race, creed and color, are you truly tapping into the maximum profitability of the company? If everyone on your team shares the same life experiences, how can your company reach the fullest potential of its capitalistic scope? This is why the key leadership principle of listening with understanding is so important. It takes input from a diverse team to reach the pinnacle of success for the company and for the members of the leadership team.

Being open to new ideas and making time to listen and develop strategies to reach specified goals is key to strong and effective leadership. It allows you to use human capital to drive profitability, build confidence in the team and empower strong leaders. Leaders must not be so busy forging their own agenda that they neglect to make time to listen. Listening to someone does not necessarily mean that the time has arrived for his or her idea. It simply means you are giving the individual a stage to build their confidence. You are empowering and inspiring by your actions and by your receptiveness.

Leaders Are Receptive

A willingness to discuss the issues at hand increases the team's confidence in the leader. Side-stepping issues does nothing but slow down the process. A strong leader has the confidence and diplomacy to step up to the plate, address a pressing issue and move on.

It takes a strong leader to support the members of the team in decisions they make. Decisions will be challenged at the upper management level and opposition will occur. It is a strong leader who can defend the hard work of the team to ultimately prevail for the good of the company, the team and the project. A strong leader is able to support the team's decisions with research, data, facts and figures. A strong leader is prepared to take a firm stand on many of the guiding principles referenced in becoming dynamic.

Leaders Delegate

A strong and effective leader has no fear in delegating responsibility to others. Whatever position of leadership you currently hold, you should be grooming someone else to take your place. Remember you are ultimately preparing to move to the next level of responsibility or promotion. This concept will be discussed more fully in the career advancement chapter. As referenced in my Pearls of Wisdom on page 54, the greatest failure in life is preventing others from accomplishing greatness. When you prevent others from becoming great, you take away from time better spent reaching your own goals. A great leader understands that they are not indispensable.

Leaders Communicate Effectively

An effective leader is consistent in words, actions and deeds. Honest and open communication in a leader is not only imperative in order to strengthen your brand, but is critical to your success and to becoming dynamic. This characteristic is of great importance in establishing your credibility. The proven value of integrity—doing what you say, saying what you mean and following through—is critical in this process. What you communicate affects what people see in you and will, in fact, determine whether people follow your lead. And consistency in communication, especially follow-up, is important. You should never have to be asked how a project is progressing; always have a clear line of communication that keeps all team members informed. The attitude of a self-starter is central to this process and is a critical characteristic in becoming dynamic.

As you become dynamic, it is your responsibility as a leader to do what you are supposed to do, when you are supposed to do it. Timeliness is a virtue. If you have deemed a project worth your time and effort, then you must value doing it right the first time. A strategic plan and deliberate execution of the plan shows your ability to organize and follow your plan to completion. If you fail to plan, failure is imminent. The impeccability of your work is critical to your success.

Be passionate at what you do and be compassionate as you execute. It takes a team to be successful, and a true leader is unselfish in giving overall credit for the team's success. A leader motivates others to follow by their ability to give credit where credit is due. A leader never loses sight of his or her commitment to the team, project or organization. Here, the leader carries the baton. It is critical that the leader remains loyal to the team members in their quest for the completion of the project.

───────

This discussion of what a strong leader is may seem overwhelming—how do I get there from where I am now? This chapter offers you the three keys to becoming a dynamic leader: substance, savvy and style. Each one is presented here with worksheets that can help you assess where you stand and what you need to do to become dynamic. If you approach leadership as a gradual process and keep your focus on continuous improvement, you will achieve your goal.

Substance

Substance is typically characterized as an intangible quality. However, *Becoming Dynamic* will be the first to discuss it from an interpersonal perspective. Substance as an interpersonal quality emphasizes the sender-receiver relationship referenced earlier. It embodies my mantra used in chapter 1, "The impact you make is the image you present." Substance is having your image reflect your values and priorities from the inside out, from how your character is expressed to how you treat others. It sets the premise of the quality needed for effective leadership. The principles of this premise are centered on leaving things in better shape than you found them, empowering people to find their strengths and inspiring confidence in others.

Substance is paramount in building your brand. It is the prerequisite for strong, effective leadership. I like to describe substance as the place where proven values, from chapter 2, and guiding principles, described below, intersect to create the dynamic leader you are intended to be.

Proven values are the intrinsic qualities that demonstrate character, and guiding principles govern how proven values are expressed in interpersonal interactions. If proven values form the essence of leadership, the addition of guiding principles completes the equation: Proven value plus guiding principles equals substance. Another way to put this is that guiding principles allow a leader to express proven values in a way that communicates substance.

Always consider guiding principles as you navigate the business arena with an eye on advancement. Individuals who consciously internalize the importance of guiding principles moves one step closer to maximizing their potential and ultimately becoming dynamic. Their colleagues and superiors will know exactly what they stand for and what to expect from their behavior.

The guiding principles that follow will clarify the guidelines that govern substantive leadership.

Defining Substance through Guiding Principles

Leadership does not necessarily occur at the upper echelons of the company. We are all leaders. Guiding principles support the development of substance that underlies your leadership skills in the workplace as well as in your community. You might ask the question, "How do I get there?" Well, if you internalize the meaning of the guiding principles that follow and envision how you use them in your daily activities of leadership, then you are well on your way to becoming dynamic. You are well on your way to increasing your self-worth, which is the foundation for much of what we have discussed thus far.

Duty is doing what you are supposed to do, when you are supposed to do it. As I alluded to in the previous chapter, I was known for completing projects before they were due to management. In my profession, juggling a flexible schedule was a challenge. It was critical that my colleagues and I were where we should be and doing what we should do, at the time it should be done. You have a duty in your commitment to the team to complete projects and follow through with consistency and fairness to all team members. It is your duty to adhere to the company guidelines. Duty parallels the proven value integrity. You have a duty to develop business relationships that are honest and above-board. It is your duty to commit to the growth and development of the people who report to you. There is no place for favoritism. You have a duty to draw a line of demarcation between personal and business relationships among team members; legal and personal ramifications could be compromised. Steer clear of these kinds of interactions. You owe it to your own authenticity as a leader.

Vision is the ability to respond proactively to changes in the market, in your industry and even in your life. Without vision, you miss the gifts that tomorrow holds. Tomorrow will come, as daybreak peeks through the clouds. Are you ready to seize the experiences that are awaiting the foresight and insight you possess? It is the visionary who has the skill to make each day anew.

It is the visionary who has the long-term plan who can weather the storms and modify the plan as conditions dictate. You do not inspire others to follow by reacting to changes as they happen. Business acumen drives vision. Business acumen is an important component of vision because it broadens your ability to create opportunity and add the value you bring to the company.

Impeccability is consistent flawless execution. Impeccability should be apparent in your pursuits. Unlike the example of the team member in Chapter 2, who was impeccably dressed but did not follow through on the same level of care and attention with his handouts, can your team count on you to execute flawlessly? Developing that critical eye is important to this process. In chapter 2, I described how watching my mother iron and flawlessly fold my father's shirts, helped me develop an eye for order and perfection. Creating a discriminating eye for detail in your work ethic is a strong asset.

Planning is essential for any endeavor. If you fail to plan, failure is imminent. Your plan coupled with your mission statement is the combination that forges business relationships. Planning is essential for any aspect of your life and career. A plan sets the course of your time frame of completion and the outcomes anticipated. Anticipated outcomes serves as the catalyst for the vision to expand your horizons. The added value that is shown in your ability to plan effectively can prove to be an asset as you prepare to advance your career. Even in the best-laid plans, failure sometimes happens. I encourage you not to give up. Failure can sometimes position you for your next success. The fact still remains, the planning process starts over. In experiencing failure, it creates benchmarks for success. It causes you to steer clear of the barriers that you experienced the first time around.

Teamwork is essential for any company or idea to reach its full potential. Diversity of thought among team members creates the synergy needed to ignite the spark that drives the fullest potential of positive results. It is ideas individually that collectively make the difference. The team makes up for any shortage of ideas or proposals that would not be reached without a homogenously diverse team. If the team is comprised of diversified race, gender and life experience, the scope of success is broadened and the benefit is increased.

Loyalty to the team and loyalty to the company is mission-critical in leadership. This is where public image plays a key role. For example, Johnson & Johnson's recognition as one of the most admired U.S. companies has much to do with industry leaders' positive dialogue about the loyalty J&J exemplifies in treatment of its employees, customers and communities. Positive words about the company and its responsibility to its employees, clients and community create an environment of loyalty. You want to create a positive environment for your team to function effectively. Creating an environment of loyalty evokes security. When employees have a feeling of security, they are more productive because of their loyalty and commitment to the company or project.

Flexibility as it relates to substantive leadership has more to do with tolerance than convenience of schedule. Flexibility is an assurance that racism, sexism, and other "isms" that drive prejudiced behavior are minimized. Flexibility breaks down the barriers that prevent amicable communication and relationships among team members. It starts from the top and spreads vertically and horizontally throughout all facets of management to provide an environment that is flexible enough to see beyond stereotypes. The stereotypes to which I refer can assassinate one's career. As stated in my Pearls of Wisdom on page 54, the greatest failure is preventing others from greatness. A substantive leader never marginalizes anyone or denies him or her opportunity to excel. The greatest failure of any team leader is to lack the flexibility of thought to see the greatness that lives inside each team member.

I want each reader to connect the dots here by asking the question, "How many times has my career taken a turn for the worse because a manager or a leader in my company had stereotypical views in mind that ultimately affected his or her impression of me?" There is responsibility on both the part of the manager/team leader and of the team member.

Becoming Dynamic: 7 Compelling Strategies for Success is the playbook that serves as the mediator of this relationship. It is the tool that offers a guide for all to strive for and become the dynamic individual you are intended to be.

Selfless service has no room for "ego." The evolution of our me-centric society and workplace leads many to live by the motto, "It's about me." Well I'm here to tell you, if you want to be a leader of substance, it's not. What you do for others is the central focus. A friend, whom I will call Laverne, once gave me a framed proverb by an unknown author that went like this: "It won't matter how big your house was. It won't matter the type car you drove. It won't matter the number of plaques on your wall. What matters is how you positively affected the life of others." Years ago, when I reflected on my sense of purpose and asked myself what my legacy would be, I realized that effectively moving someone else's career in a positive direction gives me a huge sense of accomplishment. One of the key characteristics of a leader is making sure the needs of the team are met. From carrying the baton of creating team loyalty to internalizing the substance, savvy and style that motivate others to follow, to standing behind the team in times of controversial decisions, it takes a selfless leader who looks beyond self-interest to make his or her team successful and ultimately reach its highest level of productivity.

My rationale for incorporating guiding principles is self-evident: supporting your achievement of the leadership position you seek. The only limitations that prevent many from being successful are lack of vision, passion and strong work ethic that are the driving forces of becoming dynamic. Assessing, becoming aware, and embodying guiding principles can help you make a powerful paradigm shift as you seek to be a strong and effective leader. On the worksheet on the following page, take some time to reflect on the impact of guiding principles in your life, both now and in the future.

Guiding Principles Worksheet

Review this list of guiding principles and briefly reflect on how you have manifested each principle in your life, or name a person who inspires you by embodying that principle. This exercise will bring to mind the depth of becoming dynamic and the impact made on becoming dynamic.

Guiding principle   Source of Inspiration

Duty   _____

Vision   _____

Impeccability   _____

Planning   _____

Teamwork   _____

Loyalty   _____

Flexibility   _____

Selfless Service   _____

Savvy

Savvy in leadership adds the next dimension of practical understanding of exercising kindness and consideration in the business and social setting. Etiquette, both business and social, is more than the correct placement and use of the correct knife, spoon and fork; it is the fusion of all the elements that make up a refined individual. It is yet another component in becoming dynamic. Businesses seek the best and the brightest individuals. Employers want employees who understand the importance of being able to not only work on self-managed projects, but who also possess the social skills to function effectively as a member of a team and to represent the company well. Employers seek employees who have a positive attitude and strong work ethic.

In the business, public or social setting, good manners are based on respect and genuine kindness for other people. There are many instances where selfish, inappropriate behavior dominates—failure to acknowledge a kind gesture, open conversations on the cell phone in public, disrespectful language, acting up on airplanes, and dressing in a manner that leaves much to be desired. We seem to live in a society where manners occupy a secondary role in the selfish pursuit of personal gratification. In the era of reality television shows, rudeness seems to be the norm. People model what they see. The goal of this section is to build an understanding of appropriate actions in business and in society that we can embody as leaders. In becoming dynamic every aspect of your being is on display, and you must become aware of your every action.

Manners Are Based on Respect and Consideration

Elma Hairston's Etiquette Basics

Over years of teaching classes on business etiquette as well as personal etiquette and manners, I have used these principles to explain how etiquette works. As you'll see as you read them, etiquette is nothing more than basic courtesy.

- The four most basic things to remember about manners are to say "please," "thank you," "you're welcome," and "excuse me."
- Avoid yawning or sneezing in front of others. Use a bent elbow across the face to avoid contaminating your hands. You need a clean hand to give a handshake.
- Calm prevails and gets results. Yelling to make your point never works.
- Do not walk between two people who are holding a conversation.
- Do not discuss others' shortcomings. Find something positive to say.
- Do not insult others with your words. Avoid making jokes about people.
- Be kind. You get back what you give.
- Smile more often than you frown.
- Attention to detail saves you time.

Elma Hairston's Etiquette Basics *continued*

♦ It takes more energy to judge people than to simply understand them.
♦ There is strength in being gentle.
♦ Gifts don't have to be expensive to be precious.
♦ If you are wrong and admit it, then you are right.
♦ Kindly acknowledge people in passing. Say hello.
♦ Men, gladly give up your seat to accommodate a lady.
♦ Men, remove your hat as you enter a room.
♦ Be courteous. Open the door for others.
♦ Play fair! Don't change the rules to win the game.
♦ Gossip is unacceptable. Gossip takes up time that is better spent on your own goals.
♦ Saying "no problem" is unacceptable. "You are welcome" is a gracious acknowledgment.
♦ Be gracious when you lose.
♦ Enjoy your friends and family in the special moments you share.
♦ An apology is one of life's most useful skills.
♦ Listening is one of the best gifts you can give to someone.
♦ You cannot please everybody. Be the authentic person that you are.
♦ Never call someone by their first name without permission.
♦ Make eye contact when speaking to people.
♦ Send thank you notes and birthday cards.
♦ Offer sincere compliments to others.
♦ We are the most defensive when we know we are wrong.
♦ Say thank you and smile when someone compliments you.
♦ Be mindful of the tone and selection of words when you speak.
♦ Do not be embarrassed to admit you do not know something.
♦ Nobody looks good chewing gum. Do not chew it in public. Chew gum to refresh the breath and then discard it.
♦ Never miss an opportunity to praise friends and family members.
♦ If you meet someone without a smile, give them one of yours.
♦ Do not hold a conversation on your cell phone in public.
♦ Be courteous as you travel. Think of the people in the seat behind you when reclining, be considerate with conversations, and be patient with parents with small children.
♦ Tip generously in restaurants and to bellmen, baggage handlers, taxi drivers, hairdressers, and nail technicians; they are providing valuable service.
♦ Be courteous while operating your automobile. Road rage is unacceptable.

Etiquette in some form probably began over 11,000 years ago when early humans, switching to farming from hunting and gathering, first sat down to a communal meal. The first recorded advice on manners and etiquette was written in the third millennium BC by Ptah-Hotep in the highly evolved society of ancient Egypt, more than five thousand years ago. Etiquette is a set of rules society lives by. Manners are the way society executes these rules. Over the years, I have developed the guidelines on pages 64-65 that have worked for me as a dynamic expression of proper actions that show courtesy and consideration for others. They have also helped many people who have attended my etiquette workshops to develop manners and habits that allow them to come across as poised professionals. It is by no means exclusive, but it will provide you the framework from which to build good manners and consideration for others.

A Matter of Perspective

As you embark upon each day, it is up to you to decide on the demeanor you want to personify. It is up to you to make a conscious choice to exercise courtesy and manners in all your interactions. You can take the posture of believing you can accomplish all you set out to do or you can allow a defeatist attitude to prevail. In becoming dynamic you will want to focus on creating habits that drive positive results. The glue that holds this all together is a matter of perspective. Your perspective—positive or negative—dictates your worldview. It is based upon how you view your world, your life and all that supports your reality. Much of your perspective is substantiated by the proven values that you choose to govern your life and career. Test yourself and become more aware of how your perspective affects how you interact with people and situations with the A Matter of Perspective Worksheet.

A Matter of Perspective Worksheet

The goal of this checklist is for you to become conscious of how you are presenting yourself in becoming dynamic and to motivate you to make the changes needed. On which side of the fence do you find yourself?

POSITIVE PERSPECTIVE	*NEGATIVE PERSPECTIVE*
☐ Smiles often	☐ Smiles infrequently
☐ Willing to change ideas, dress and behavior, when appropriate	☐ Resistant to change
☐ Accepting of others' perspectives	☐ Refuse to see others' points of view
☐ Rarely complains	☐ Consistently complains
☐ Admits when wrong	☐ Blames others
☐ Rarely criticizes others	☐ Very critical of others
☐ Considerate of others	☐ Thinks of self and "what's in it for me?"
☐ Takes responsibility for actions	☐ Makes excuses
☐ Receptive of others' ideas and opinions	☐ Forces ideas and opinions on others

Style

Creating your individual style appropriate to your industry is a defining component of becoming dynamic. It will earn you respect and open doors to advancement. My mother used to say, "Dress like a million dollars and people will respect you in the same way." This is an old adage from the past, but the meaning is relevant today. Even if you do not have a million dollars, dressing with class and purpose nets you respect that might otherwise be withheld. People may withhold their respect because you do not exemplify trust, integrity and confidence in your presentation.

Dress for the Position You Seek, Not for the Position You Hold

The style you create should be done with deliberate thought in mind. It speaks to your self-worth and enhances your effectiveness in business. My mother used to say, "If you feel like you look your best, you will perform at your best." It is a mindset that drives the success factor. Your style not only communicates who you are, but, depending on your selection of attire, it dictates the position you aspire to achieve. Proven values should be apparent in your style—integrity, credibility, impeccability and honesty. Your style should be consistent and differentiate you from your peers. Excellence is just as important here as it is in any aspect of what we have communicated.

Select Colors That Complement Your Style and Extract a Positive Response

We live in a visual society; images that we perceive as positive motivate us to action. Believe it or not, the colors you wear influence emotion and extract a positive or negative response. The psychology of color is a rich field of research. Having knowledge of this gives you direction on selecting colors that not only complement your style, but that extract a positive response. (See the Psychology of Color, on the following page.)

Fabric selection is also important when defining your style. You will want to select fabrics that contain natural fibers like linen, wool gabardine, worsted wool or cotton. Blends work, but there should be a percentage of natural fiber. These are basic guidelines that will guide you in becoming dynamic and creating a leadership style that motivates others to follow. More specific guidance will follow.

The Psychology of Color

➤ Red	⟷	Exciting, vibrant, aggressive
➤ Orange	⟷	Cheerful, warm, energetic
➤ Green	⟷	Calm, fresh, balanced
➤ Yellow	⟷	Bright, sunny, warm
➤ Blue	⟷	Peaceful, tranquil, authoritative
➤ Purple	⟷	Royal, powerful, dignified
➤ White		Innocent, youthful, pure
➤ Gray	⟷	Modest, mature, conservative
➤ Brown	⟷	Balance, warmth, approachable
➤ Navy Blue	⟷	Professional, confident, trustworthy
➤ Gold	⟷	Wealthy, prosperous, courageous
➤ Black	⟷	Power, elegance, formality

Attire Should Be Appropriate for Your Industry

In considering the appropriate attire for your specific industry, strive for a balance between a look that propels you to success and a look not worthy of a second glance. That means you don't want a style that says, "Look at me!" You want a style that says, "My appearance reflects my self-respect, integrity, and ambition." The professions in which you want to be more conservative would consist of law, banking, accounting and professional sales. Professions that would dictate a less conservative style would be marketing, sales, retail, education, real estate, and engineering. More flexibility can be exercised in artistic professions like public relations, art, advertising and interior design.

Basic Office Wardrobe Checklist

FOR MEN	FOR WOMEN

Suit basics
  ➤ Navy blue suit
  ➤ Charcoal blue/grey suit
  ➤ Black suit (optional; an alternative for formal wear)
	Suit basics
	  ➤ Navy-blue suit
	  ➤ Black dress
	  ➤ Well-tailored pantsuit

Shirts
  ➤ Two textured fabric shirts (pin stripe, mixed pattern)
  ➤ Two white shirts (one with French cuffs/one without)
  ➤ One light blue shirt (your choice French cuffs or not)
	Shirts/blouses
	  ➤ Blouse with collar in white, soft pink, soft tan, light blue
	  ➤ Simple tank (not a plunging neckline)

Ties
  ➤ One plain silk tie
  ➤ One textured/pattern tie
	Shoes
	  ➤ Closed toe pumps in navy, beige, or black

Shoes
  ➤ One black pair lace-up shoes
  ➤ One black pair slip-on shoes
  ➤ One brown pair shoes (your choice of hue)
	Hose and shapewear
	  ➤ Hosiery (sheer and opaque)
	  ➤ Undergarments that shape with no unsightly lines

Accessories
  ➤ Cufflinks/silver and gold
  ➤ Black belt (silver buckle/gold buckle)
  ➤ Socks (solid color, coordinated to suit; calf or knee high)
  ➤ Black leather briefcase or nylon computer bag
	Accessories
	  ➤ Scarves
	  ➤ Single strand of pearls
	  ➤ Gold/silver-tone necklace
	  ➤ Earrings (small to medium), gold, silver or pearls
	  ➤ All-weather coat (trench coat)

There is a language that speaks to the response that the style that you create evokes. A jacket worn with a blouse or shirt with a collar suggests authority or that you're in an upper management position. You want to dress for the position you seek, not for the position you hold. A basic two-piece suit or dress with no more than moderate cleavage is appropriate. Running shoes in the office are an insult. Invest in a comfortable, stylish pair of flat shoes instead. For men, lace-up shoes or wing tips are good choices. Closed-toe pumps for women, with no more than a two-inch heel, are appropriate for business attire. Rule of thumb: there is safety in conservatism if you are not sure as to the attire. In professional sales, parallel how your customers dress.

Women's and men's hairstyles and accessories should also mirror your industry standard. Observe people around you. Keep abreast of the people who are shakers and movers in the company. Observe the types of hairstyles being worn by those whose careers are moving. Here, I would follow the lead of those whose careers are moving to higher levels of responsibility.

Women should be mindful of fingernail length, color of nail polish, and the number of rings displayed on the fingers. If there is a question, opt for less; excessive ornamentation can look unprofessional and distract from your message. A conservative nail length, neutral nail polish, and one ring on the left-hand ring finger and one ring on the right-hand ring finger is acceptable in the business arena. Your message will be lost if people pay more attention to your ornamentation than to your words.

I spent ten (10) years in the banking industry with First Interstate Bank (now Wells Fargo). My career started in trust and estate administration and culminated in the management-training program. Although the financial services industry did not become my life's work, I learned some valuable lessons from many who shaped my career. A vice-president whom I will call Mary A. was a statuesque, well-dressed woman. She had a conservative hairstyle, and would wear a navy blue suit with an open-collar, crisp white blouse, and closed-toe two-inch heels. She was the epitome of the corporate woman. As a neophyte, I could not afford the quality of her wardrobe, but I took note and began to place some conscious effort in purchasing clothes and creating a style consistent with Mary A., including her hairstyle. As confirmed by my performance reviews, the management team noticed. My work ethic was described as superior and my character, reputation and image as exemplary. I was approached to become a part of the management-training program.

How I presented myself removed many of the deep-rooted stereotypes around women's ability to reflect the corporate culture. Using your image to break down stereotypes is mission-critical, not only for yourself, but to pave a clear path for others. If it takes dressing in a manner that fits your industry, if it takes wearing your hairstyle in a manner that is industry specific, you would do well to follow this advice. Remember: You cannot effectively change anything from the outside looking in. You must be on the inside where change is being made to make an impact for yourself and others.

Creating Your Style

Don't be intimidated by putting together a dynamic work wardrobe. Begin by building on what you already have. Start by organizing your closet, identifying pieces that would work in your business environment and coordinating patterns and pieces. Fill gaps by investing in classic clothes, especially pieces with flattering vertical lines. If your budget is limited, plan your wardrobe around separates that can work in multiple ways. This is especially effective if you work with basic colors such as navy, white, red and beige. However much you spend, focus on quality, natural fibers, and proper fit.

Other areas of your appearance are critical, as well. Attention to skin care and dental hygiene demonstrates self-respect. Facial hair for men should be neat and well groomed, close to the face. Women should have manageable hairstyles that are suitable for the workplace.

Investment Shopping vs. Occasion Shopping

Investment shopping is purchasing for the long term. It is purchasing clothes that you can transition from business to business casual and from business professional to after-five simply by adding or removing accessories that do not fit the event. Investment shopping in the long run is a money-saving measure because you are planning your wardrobe instead of buying on impulse. Occasion shopping is just that, impulse purchasing. Without a plan and without a sense of your lifestyle, business goals and social interactions, you leave yourself vulnerable to spending more than you intend. You will blow your budget before you realize it, and other expenses will suffer.

Following is a series of basic guidelines that will help you build a wardrobe that will support your quest to become dynamic.

Business Casual Attire

Business casual has become the norm for Fridays, a way of easing into the weekend, as well as for some business meetings. While it is more comfortable than a suit and tie, don't fool yourself that there isn't a dress code in force. Line up relaxed clothing that is appropriate to conduct business in a professional manner and in the environment conducive to conduct business (appropriate for the office, not a golf course or a ski resort). Again, pay attention to the standard followed in your work setting. Some companies may welcome jeans or chinos, while others frown on them. Whatever your choices, be sure you look fresh and tailored—no rips, obvious labels, glitter or logos. Use common sense and good judgment—your image and reputation are at stake.

Business Casual Checklist

FOR MEN	FOR WOMEN
➢ Transitional sports jacket or blazer worn with • Open-collar shirt • Polo shirt • Mock turtleneck ➢ Chinos ➢ Jeans, if allowed ➢ Relaxed dress slacks ➢ Urban Suave™ (depending on industry) ➢ Slip-on shoes, athletic shoes, if allowed ➢ Accessories • Cufflinks (silver and gold) • Black belt (silver/gold buckle) • Socks (solid color, coordinated to attire; calf or knee high) • Nylon computer bag	➢ Blazer or cardigan worn with • Blouse • Pullover sweater • Twin set • Mock turtle neck ➢ Slacks or a skirt ➢ Tailored dress with on-trend overtones ➢ Don't forget hosiery and shape wear (women on the move wear hosiery in the business setting) ➢ Avoid plunging necklines • Blouse, jacket, slacks • V-Neck or round neck pull-over, tank style top, jacket, slacks ➢ Jewelry: gold, silver, pearls ➢ Slip-ons or closed-toe flats (no sandals or athletic shoes)

Office to Casual Elegant

A subset of business casual is "dress-down Friday." At the end of a long week, what is better than going out with your colleagues to relax, socialize, listen to some music and get out on the dance floor? While your get-down-and-party outfit might be too edgy for the office, you can build on your casual Friday basics with bolder accessories, shoes, and jewelry. For example, if your office dress code allows jeans, you can adopt an Urban Suave™ look by knotting your tie at lower-chest height and switching out your sports coat for a leather jacket. You can trade your two-inch heels for platform sandals and your gold stud earrings for dramatic hoops. The Dress-Down Friday to Casual

Elegant Checklist gives examples of how you can transform your look that takes you from the office to the weekend.

Dress-Down Friday to Casual Elegant Checklist

FOR MEN	FOR WOMEN
➤ Urban Suave™: jacket and shirt with necktie knotted at lower chest, jeans	➤ Transitional jacket
➤ Boat shoes or slip-ons	➤ Tank top (not too revealing)
➤ Raw silk crew neck or v-neck sweater (white or neutral colors)	➤ Jeans (not too restricting)
➤ Open collar shirt (no tie) or with tie (urban suave style)	➤ Black dress
➤ Neutral jacket (black & blue herringbone or black & brown herringbone)	➤ Slip-on flats or pumps (no flip-flops or athletic shoes)
	➤ Mix and match as venue dictates
	➤ Jewelry with flair

Attire for Formal/Social Events and Parties

Attending social/formal events and parties provide another opportunity to leverage your substance, savvy and style. The invitation will usually state the attire, but the basic guidelines for formal/social events and parties deserve some clarity.

Let me preface this entire section by saying that for women, St. John knits can be worn in any category depending on the event, from formal embellished styles to less formal without the embellishment.

Black Tie suggests a very formal event. For men, a tuxedo is a must for your wardrobe, worn with a crisp, starched white shirt with a wing collar or tuxedo collar. Add a black bow tie, silk ascot, or navy or black necktie. Black shoes are a must; they can be either slip on or tie-up black formal shoes in patent leather or soft leather. In spring and summer, you can replace the black tuxedo jacket with a white tuxedo jacket over black trousers.

Black tie for women suggests a floor-length formal evening dress worn with a more formal shoe embellished with jewels or plain toe. High heels or a sandal with diagonal or vertical straps is appropriate, as well. You have a great deal of flexibility in dress style and color, so wear the color and style that accent your stature and figure. Be sure to wear appropriate undergarments to create a smooth, well put-together, classy look. The amount and style of jewelry truly depends on the dress. So give some deliberate thought as to whether to wear a necklace and earrings together, but earrings are an important detail. Women have a great deal of flexibility with earring styles, especially whether they are embellished with jewels or not. Earrings can dangle one to two inches below the earlobe; however, wearing earrings close to the ear is a current trend. Neck jewelry is dependent on the neckline, which should be modest, without revealing too much cleavage. A round neckline might call for a choker or solid chain, a V-neckline pendant, and a high-necked dress might need no neck jewelry at all. Again, it depends on the dress and the occasion. When you put together your look, keep in mind that less is more. Are you comfortable with the amount of cleavage? Does your jewelry complement the dress, not overwhelm it? If you look in the mirror and feel uncomfortable with the look you have created, then back to the drawing board.

After Five or Semi-Formal suggests an event that is less formal in attire, however, it calls for the same attention to detail as black-tie. As it suggests it is usually after 5 p.m. in the evening. Men can wear a tuxedo, as described above, or a black suit with a black necktie, along with a crisp medium starch white shirt. Shoe style stated above. A white dinner jacket is appropriate, as well. It is also acceptable for men to wear a formal white starched wing collar shirt worn without a tie. A silk crewneck T-shirt can be matched with a tuxedo jacket and still meet the same level of dress code.

For women, After Five or Semi-Formal calls for a dress that is knee length, slightly above the knee, or tea length (reaching the calf). Your choice of jewelry and shoes is the same as formal attire, described above.

Black Tie Optional suggests an event that is less formal and allows flexibility in attire. It is a mixture of formal and semi-formal for both men and women.

Casually Elegant suggests a more relaxed elegant look. Men can wear a tuxedo jacket with a crisp medium starched white open-collar shirt, or preferably a black, navy or charcoal-gray suit. In the spring and summer, a lighter color suit is acceptable. In warmer climates, however, a lighter color linen or seersucker suit is acceptable year-round. Shoes should coordinate, depending on the look you choose. Shoes can be slip-ons, dock shoes or loafers.

For women, after five or semi-formal attire is totally appropriate for a casually elegant event. A dinner suit, which is a bit dressier than a typical business suit, can be worn as well. Typical dinner suit fabrics can be silk shantung, embellished with a raised pattern, or a St. John-style knit. Shoes can be selected from above. Jewelry accessories can be selected from above, as well.

White Party Chic suggests a theme-party atmosphere reserved for spring, summer or early fall. It is critically important that you follow this dress code with uninterrupted white attire. Typically the fabric worn is white linen or other white fabric deemed appropriate for the occasion. Undergarments should be flesh tone or white, never black. Black undergarments underneath white takes on a gray hue. Shoes should be white for both men and women. Please respect the request of the host by adhering to the theme. Do not add accent colors. Jewelry should be pearls (women) or gold or silver tone for men and women.

Here are some "pearls of wisdom" for refining your style. I have developed them over my twenty-five-year career, and I know they work. I share them with you to help you achieve becoming dynamic in your pursuit of leading with substance, savvy and style.

Pearls of Wisdom (Men)

- ➤ Dressing with confidence prevails
- ➤ Facial hair shadowed close to face
- ➤ Match the length and style of your hair to your industry
- ➤ Pant length stops at your shoe heel
- ➤ Jacket stops at your wrist bone
- ➤ Shirt cuff stops at your thumb bone
- ➤ Necktie coordinates/contrasts with shirt and suit
- ➤ Wear a white T-shirt under a dress shirt at all times

Pearls of Wisdom (Women)

- ➤ Use your wardrobe to express confidence rather than marginalizing your position: vertical lines, tailored jacket, collared blouse, conservative dress with sleeves (cap, 3/4 length, long sleeves, etc.)
- ➤ Choose your wardrobe based on your industry or career
- ➤ Follow fashion trends with conservative overtones
- ➤ Management: rely on business suits, tailored dresses
- ➤ Sales/Marketing: knits & two-piece dresses are acceptable
- ➤ A shirt or blouse with a collar reflects expertise, credibility
- ➤ Avoid extremes of patterns and styles that distract
- ➤ No spandex or leggings for the office (too informal)
- ➤ Sleeveless dresses must be approached with caution: You want attention on your message, not your skin

What Does Your Body Language Say?

On your journey to becoming dynamic, you have taken the message of Substance, Savvy, and Style to heart. You have examined your values, polished up your manners and attitude toward others, and invested time and money in your wardrobe. Now here's the icing on the cake: Are you aware of the impact of your body language?

Nonverbal communication is as important as what you say. Mannerisms speak volumes when interacting in the business environment. The following will offer some guidance in the interpretation of mannerisms that can enhance your image or detract from your road to becoming dynamic.

What Does Your Body Language Say?

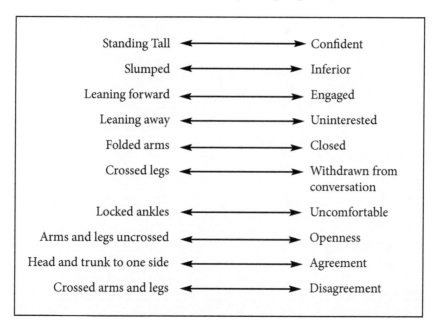

Standing Tall	←——————→	Confident
Slumped	←——————→	Inferior
Leaning forward	←——————→	Engaged
Leaning away	←——————→	Uninterested
Folded arms	←——————→	Closed
Crossed legs	←——————→	Withdrawn from conversation
Locked ankles	←——————→	Uncomfortable
Arms and legs uncrossed	←——————→	Openness
Head and trunk to one side	←——————→	Agreement
Crossed arms and legs	←——————→	Disagreement

Body language can be broken down into a variety of elements that communicate your mood and attitude. Elements of communication can be broken down into your posture, how you control your facial expression and make eye contact, your gestures, spatial awareness, and how you use your voice. How you control these elements has an impact on others' first impressions of you and influence how they perceive you in the workplace. Learning to be aware of and manage these elements is key to becoming dynamic and opening up opportunities.

Elements of Communication

Voice	Posture
➢ Inflection/Pitch ➢ Intensity ➢ Rate ➢ Faulty Pronunciation ➢ Poor Articulation ➢ Don't Use "Uh" as a Filler Word. Pause Instead	➢ Stand tall ➢ Head up ➢ Shoulders square
Space	**Messages**
➢ Territory/Comfort Zone ➢ Culturally Designed ➢ Mixed Gender ➢ Communicates Level of the Relationship	➢ Firm Hand Shake –Appropriate ➢ Hugging – Inappropriate in the business setting ➢ Touching at the Waist – Inappropriate in the business setting
Facial Expressions ➢ Happiness ➢ Sadness ➢ Anger ➢ Disgust ➢ Surprise ➢ Fear **Eye Contact** ➢ Mirror to your person ➢ Character revealed ➢ Confidence ➢ Sincerity	**Gestures** ➢ Illustrate and Reinforce the Message ➢ Involves Various Parts of the Body Working in Concert ➢ Verbal and Non-Verbal Message ➢ Openness – Palms Up ➢ Reinforce a Point – Upturned Fist ➢ Trustworthiness – Tight Hand Shake ➢ Agreement – Thumbs Up ➢ Negative Attitude – Clinched Fists ➢ Deceit – Touching Nose ➢ Nervousness – Pacing Back & Forth ➢ Suspicion – Pulling at Your Collar

The goal of this chapter was to build an awareness of the important space that substance, savvy and style occupies in becoming dynamic. Leading with substance, savvy and style is a unique and verified concept. As you follow the guidelines here to strengthen your image and your brand, you want to be consistent in all you do, whether in or outside the office, as your "presence in motion" evolves. As you attend your team's evening dinners or office parties, presence in motion and professionalism should remain at the top of your mind. Your image is on display, and your brand can either be strengthened or weakened. Leading with substance, savvy and style is the trademark of the refined leader ready to embark upon the challenges ahead.

4

Building Strategic Relationships

Consistency Drives the Dynamics of Confidence

A YOUNG LADY, WHOM I will call Emma, approached me after a workshop for business professionals that I facilitated. Her concern was that although she had a master's degree and the skill set to qualify her for more responsibility on her job, she stood on the sidelines while her coworkers were promoted. She informed me that few of her coworkers had college degrees; most had a high school diploma or technical school certificate. She could not understand why they were progressing and she was not. After having her respond to the Before You Start questionnaire on page 19, we clearly defined the first problem—the absence of a strategic and deliberate approach to building business relationships. Based on her responses and our discussion, we identified the things she needed to address in order to build the relationships that would help her advance in her career.

Business Relationships Built on Trust Inspire Confidence

As you progress through the journey of becoming dynamic, you will encounter themes of consistency and trust. Consistency and trust are the guiding principles for decision making. They are the cornerstone of becoming dynamic.

Business relationships are based on consistency in words, actions, deeds and professional presentation. As we have discussed in earlier chapters, consistency in your professional presentation leads to trust. Trust ignites the confidence on which relationships are built. It positions you for more successful business endeavors, which ultimately advances you to higher levels of accomplishments. As managers gain confidence in the consistency you bring in your work ethic, professional presentation and overall ability to represent the company or project, you will inspire their trust.

You set the stage for whether your colleagues and managers trust you. Eighty percent of the time, people determine whether they will build a relationship with you before you utter a word. It is your image that motivates others to follow. It is your image that builds the foundation of becoming dynamic. It is the visual presentation that sends a positive or negative message about you.

For individuals to maximize their image, they must develop a mission statement and professional plan centered on forging business relationships and career advancement.

Before I return to the story of Emma, let me share another experience that underscores the importance of consistency and trust. Renee, the manager of a benefits processing department, was promoted to this position because her manager communicated to her, "I can always count on you to represent the company well when we have visits from upper management from New York, even on casual Fridays." This statement reflects the trust factor involved in building relationships internally. In becoming dynamic, relationships are built both internally and externally. External relationships will be covered in chapter 7, Community Service.

Renee's story is an example of how trust and confidence propelled her career to higher levels of responsibility. A clear understanding of expectations from both manager and employee is critical for success. The lack of clear interpretation of expectations is a major drawback in career advancement.

With Emma, to meet her goal of building business relationships and inspiring trust, we identified three objectives. The first was to improve the impression she made, the second was to leverage her strong qualities, and third was to develop a plan for advancement within the company. The Before You Start questionnaire was utilized to provide direction and clarity to her path to success. Articulating the answers identified the need to emphasize diplomacy and voice inflection, which called attention to the tone, pitch and speed as she speaks.

Utilizing the format of role-playing prepared Emma for real-life execution. Role-playing allows an individual to rehearse responses that might otherwise be omitted because of lack of readiness in a given situation. This is not to suggest you should adopt a robotic style of delivery. It is to prepare you with intelligent and compelling responses. I call this deliberate execution. In the real-life situation, you may include additional dialogue, but the core of your message will be well-thought out and you will be ready for any challenges that might arise.

Without meaning to, Emma projected an intimidating demeanor that impeded her progress in developing positive working relationships. She seldom smiled and acted as if she had a chip on her shoulder. Her coworkers went so far as to inform their manager that they were afraid to approach her. Her verbal approach was sound and articulate, but lacked diplomacy. In addition, the colors in her wardrobe did not complement her style, nor did her clothing style parallel the advancement goals she had for her career. These are just some of the aesthetics that impacted her need to enhance her professional presentation, verbally and nonverbally. In short, she had the education to propel her career, but she lacked the soft skills and the image that it takes to reach the goals we identified for her.

I will allow you, the reader, to determine if there were other considerations at play. Did her coworkers resent her advanced education? Were there cultural differences? Was there another form of bias at play? Can you relate to this scenario? I ask you to be the judge. The questions in the Before You Start questionnaire on how to handle ethnicity paints a broad picture; it is prudent to give some conscious thought to this question. Attitudes toward ethnicity are the elephant in the room that many times no one wants to address. However, I suggest that you use the strategic and deliberate content of this book to rise above the mediocrity of those who let their biases get in the way of supporting their coworkers.

Remember: "One of the greatest failures in life is preventing others from becoming great." If you do not feel confident in the presence of those who you perceive to have more to offer than you in the way of education or any other characteristics, for that matter, then it is incumbent upon you to develop a plan of action to achieve the level of success that makes you feel complete. Creating barriers to the success of others should not be the method of operation. Becoming dynamic is one tool that can be utilized to achieve the authenticity of your greatness, so you do not feel threatened by those you perceive who have reached theirs.

It is prudent at this point to chronicle Emma's wardrobe faux pas so that you can draw your own conclusion about your wardrobe. If image and wardrobe is a goal for you, then enjoy the ride. We used the basic wardrobe guide in chapter 3 to perform an inventory of her wardrobe. We discussed the look she wanted to achieve and agreed on the methods used to reach her goal. She had been wearing colors and patterns that did not complement her figure or stature, in partic- ular a brown jacket with a brown tank top worn underneath, which did not flatter her skin tone and made her look drab. We started by framing her face with a contrasting collared blouse. A collared blouse is a subconscious cue that suggests authority. We chose white, soft pink, and beige. We added a strand of pearls. We also focused on jackets that tapered just below her hips, which added strength to her stature. Her dresses included horizontal patterns that did not complement her 5'2" stature. Our goal was to add height by creating a longer line to her stature. We selected solid colors with vertical lines in order to add height. We achieved our goal by adding accessories that complemented her stature and that created an image of confidence and approachability. We used the psychology of color chart to consciously select colors that bring about a positive response. The end result was a professional look that projected a sense of self-worth, approachable authority and professionalism.

We assessed her impact, utilizing the What Is Your Impact? (page 24) and A Matter of Perspective (page 67) worksheets to help her understand how others perceived her.

Now let's execute the plan. The first objective of the plan was to package Emma in a way that empowered her but did not intimidate others.

We did a color analysis and wardrobe assessment to determine the best color combinations and styles based on her height and stature, referenced above. We worked on her posture and mannerisms, as spelled out in chapter 3. A trip to her dentist gave her the confidence of a bright, inviting smile.

The second objective was to leverage and build on Emma's strong qualities, uncovered in her Before You Start questionnaire. Each morning as she walked into the office, she greeted each coworker with a positive word and a smile by simply being cordial. She consistently exemplified this behavior by exhibiting a positive attitude (identified by the worksheets mentioned above). Her new attitude and professional presentation strengthened her brand and built solid relationships.

She also changed her mode of communicating. For example, instead of summary statements such as "I see it this way..." and yes/no questions, which do not promote dialogue, she introduced clarifying, open-ended questions such as "How do you... "What do you..." "What is your understanding..." These open-ended questions furthered dialogue and promoted understanding among Emma and her colleagues. Some of the phrases she used in communicating with her manager were: "What are the job specifications for this position?" "How will I be evaluated on performance?" "When is the evaluation period?" She used questions that point to clarity.

The third problem we identified was that she had no plan of action in place for moving to the position she wanted to achieve and for forging the relationships that she needed to make this happen.

Again, Emma took her responses to the Before You Start questionnaire and used them to create her plan, which included a Value Proposition Statement (page 90), which integrates her power words, her proven values, and her professional mission statement. This accomplished two things: she had a strategic plan focused on her goals, as well as a deliberate method of execution by developing talking points to communicate her career goals. Emma was now well on her way to becoming dynamic.

Over the next few months, Emma was empowered by her new level of self-awareness. Her self-confidence was boosted by her more professional look. She began to dress for the position she wanted, not for the position she currently held. Once she broke down the barriers of communication, her coworkers began asking her for help on projects that her demeanor did not give them permission to ask in the past. Her true ability began to emerge among her coworkers.

She met with the department manager for her six-month evaluation. The dialogue opened with positive feedback he had received from her coworkers, a marked difference from past communication. She was armed with a succinct statement defining her proven values, goals and mission statement, thanks to having developed her Value Proposition.

This would have been the time for Emma to identify a mentor and a sponsor within the company who could guide her in seeking a promotion, because she had strengthened her relationships and her support system. Instead, another corporation offered her a position that was commensurate with her degree and skill set. This put her well on the way to advancing her career. Emma had been empowered to make the necessary adjustments and ultimately positioned herself for a bright future. She has continued to be successful in her business career and still utilizes the skills of strategically planning and deliberately executing strong and sustaining business relationships.

Your vision statement and value proposition forms the roadmap that provides direction as you move toward accomplishing your goals. It lays the groundwork for the passion, preparation, practice performance, and polish that provide the rationale in your pursuits, which has been previously expounded upon.

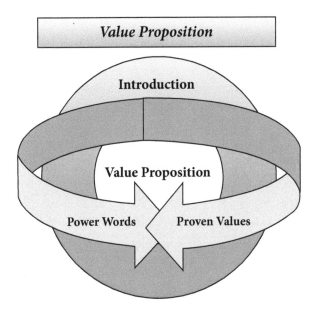

Power Words and Proven Values

How many times have you been asked to introduce yourself at a networking event or company meeting? I have observed many who ramble on and on, hoping that something was said that made an impact. No longer will you feel insecure about your message. No longer will your message be without focus or purpose. "Make them want more" by providing a focused and powerful message about you that will have a lasting effect.

When developing your story, introductions should start with your name, company position and your reason for creating this moment. Next, select words from the Power Words worksheet in chapter 1 to describe your persona. Add your Proven Values from chapter 2. Then you will want to state your passion, your legacy or the contribution you want to make. The composite of your value proposition, not only gives you direction as to your mission and vision, but also strengthens your brand.

My Value Proposition Statement

Name: _____

Title or Job Responsibility:_____

Company Name: _____

Power words to use in introducing yourself: principled, drive, determination, tenacity
Proven values to use to introduce yourself: integrity, excellence, commitment, work ethic

Mission Statement: Connects present goals to future outcomes.

_____

_____

_____

_____

Vision Statement: Connects future goals to outcomes over time.

_____

_____

_____

_____

Here are some examples to get you started:

> My name is E. J. Hairston. I am Founder and Managing Director of Dynamic Images International LLC. I am principled with the drive, determination and tenacity to succeed. (*mission statement*) My purpose in life is to fulfill my passion of motivating others by utilizing my skill of public speaking. (*vision statement*)

Depending upon your career direction, here are other examples showing how you can personalize the statement:

> My name is _____. My goal is to become an Information Technology Engineer (*mission statement*) in order to develop new and innovative technology for the IT industry. (vision statement)

> My name is _____. My goal is to become a lawyer (*mission statement*) to fulfill my passion of becoming a voice for the voiceless. (*vision statement*)

Conscious Effort Is Key in Building Business Relationship

Do you remember going over the questions in the Before You Start questionnaire? They can be customized to your individual situation. As you answer each question, make a determination as to which questions are relevant to your individual situation. It may be one or two or it may be all. The choice is yours depending on the goals you want to achieve. Then use the information to create your own Value Proposition statement. If you haven't filled out the Before You Start questionnaire yet, go back and do it now.

In order to forge strong business relationships, you must first understand the art of *building* these relationships. In order to become dynamic, it takes strategic planning and deliberate execution in building strong and sustaining relationships. It is these relationships that have a direct impact on you and securing your place among your peers and upper management.

Emma's experience shows how an individual becomes dynamic through honest self-examination and clear articulation of her goals.

I challenge you to take a moment to invest some time in this process of introspection. You will be amazed what you accomplish. You will be amazed at the impact it has on your success and your ultimate, becoming dynamic.

5

Finessing Your Success

Leveraging Your Dynamic Strengths for Growth

ACHIEVING THE PINNACLE OF your success does not happen without deliberate and strategic thought. Success is achieved by developing a plan that is focused on vision, hard work, drive, determination and tenacity. Success can be preceded by equivocation, uncertainty and fear. However, dynamic, successful people manage these feelings by maintaining a positive attitude. A positive attitude is the foundation of success and provides the motivation to persevere. Perseverance is the guiding principle that motivates dynamic people to remain steadfast in their commitment to their mission statement and the goals set out in their plan of action. I call this "finessing the success factor" — pushing through barriers and setbacks and making the extra effort that ensures your success.

Elma Hairston's Plan for Success

To Achieve Success	Position Yourself for Success	Plan for Success
➢ Uncover and follow your passion ➢ Understand your purpose ➢ Positive attitude is the foundation for success	➢ Push through barriers and setbacks ➢ Exert the extra effort to ensure success ➢ Exclude negative people from your circle of influence	➢ Stay committed to your mission statement and goals ➢ Study successful people ➢ Review and modify your plan often

In his poem, "Harlem," Langston Hughes, who has been called the Poet Laureate of Harlem, states, "What happens to a dream deferred? Does it dry up like a raisin in the sun?" (1951). I say to you: Never let anyone stand in the way of your dreams. Never give up; never give in. You can, you will, you must have all there is for you in life. I have had a very successful career, but I also experienced challenges that caused me to question my purpose. I want to share part of my story to help you understand how I kept my focus on ultimate success and did not accept that a current setback would be the end of the story.

You Are More Than a Conqueror

There are so many people who live their lives in what I call the "should have, could have, would have" syndrome. Do not defer what you should be focusing on today for lack of a plan to execute for tomorrow. Tomorrow may never come. Let's be honest. Life gets in the way. As life gets in the way, press on. "The race is not given to the swift or strong, but to those who endure to the end" (Ecclesiastes 9:11).

Another scripture that motivates me to achieve is found in Romans 8:35–38, "You are more than a conqueror." It is through your preparation for the task that makes you more than a conqueror. You will allow nothing to stand in the path that has been set forth for you. It is strong and sustaining business relationships that make you more than a conqueror. It is your professional image that makes you more than a conqueror. In becoming dynamic, it is your faith that makes you more than a conqueror. Utilize all the talent and resources you have to give your best effort in all of your pursuits.

As I reflect upon past experiences, my goal is to inspire you to persevere if you encounter frustration in your pursuit. I have been president or committee chair of numerous community, church, political and civic organizations. I was appointed to these positions, I believe, because people saw in me the characteristics of a strong leader encompassing substance, savvy and style. In fulfilling the duties of the group leader, it was discouraging to plan for a productive meeting and encounter individuals with agendas that are not specific to making the organization strong, but to advance their own interests. My strategy was to develop an internal support system within the group that minimize these actions so that the goals of the organization were met despite of the barriers. When you experience a similar situation, you must internalize that it is only temporary. You have the proven values and guiding principles to weather the storm. Have you ever observed that after a storm, the sun shines? This is how life works. Barriers may be placed in the path to your success, but if you just hold to your proven values and guiding principles, you will be successful.

I am not just reinforcing ideas that I explained in the previous chapters of this book. I am communicating what I have lived to be able to share with you those experiences, values and principles that have strengthened my fortitude to share with you. I am still standing even after hurtful words and actions. I am more than a conqueror because I did not allow those words to stand in the way of my dreams.

When you take on leadership roles, you will encounter people from different cultures, backgrounds and life experiences. It is important to exercise empathy as we move forward in meeting our goals. As we examine our differences, we must also consider the common ground on which we all stand. That common ground demands that we should walk a mile in someone else's shoes so we can understand what they endure.

Using Setbacks for Growth

My dream of becoming an image consultant was deferred early in my pursuit of this career objective. In 1996, my good friend, whom I will call Linda, allowed me to present my first attempt at wardrobe consultation and color analysis to a group of women at her home. I was so excited. The presentation went extremely well. Since this was before PowerPoint, I used charts that mapped out the basic colors. I also provided the women with a list of the elements of a basic wardrobe. I demonstrated combinations of attire to meet specific objectives. This is where I introduced the concept of investment shopping. By most accounts, the women communicated to me that they had never heard many of the points I brought to mind, and they found them very relevant. I offered many examples of how to enhance their professional career by enhancing their wardrobe.

Wouldn't you know it, I overheard one woman say, "Who is she to tell us how to dress? She is no authority on the subject." By all accounts, my image and attire reflected the message and strengthened my brand—in contrast to her attitude and demeanor, which left much to be desired. I allowed these discouraging words to defer my dream. They caused me to question my expertise. I let her negativity have more power over me, at the time, than the encouragement from the other women. You must consider the source of the words. They were spoken by a woman who needed my counsel on the subject of professional image, yet was so insecure about herself that she felt she needed to put me down. Still, for many years I allowed these words to lay dormant in my psyche.

Moments in life like this one lead you to examine yourself and take action. I set out on a mission to make sure no one questioned my expertise or authenticity on the subject matter of professional image. I have spent a lifetime of achieving, sharpening my skill and developing my expertise. I offer workshops for business professionals and young people that help them in their own quest to become dynamic. Now, as I write this book, I am living out my destiny: "I am more than a conqueror." I have strengthened my skill, my expertise and my person through much of what you have experienced thus far in this book. As I revise the chapters of this book, the compelling realization hits me that it chronicles a very personal journey to becoming dynamic. My goal is to make my journey your journey.

Positioning Yourself for Success

Success is achieved by an indwelling desire to succeed: "Anything worth having is worth working for." The desire to succeed was placed inside you to inspire you to act. It is your actions coupled with drive, determination and tenacity that bring your success to fruition. These actions can be in the form of a plan, where you build networks and support systems. These actions can be extrapolated from the power words you worked on in chapter 2 and from the other tools and methods that you acquire as you incorporate the content of this book into your own life. As you ponder your success, power words motivate and invigorate. Positioning you for success is the goal. Developing a mental posture is your role.

This anonymous poem, titled "Success," captures some of the benchmarks of success that have motivated me to higher levels of accomplishment. It goes beyond status or self-serving displays.

> Success is measured by
> the height of your aspirations
> the breadth of your vision
> the depth of your convictions
> Success lies not in how well-known you are
> But how well-respected
> Not in the power to take
> But in your willingness to give
> —*Author unknown*

The height of your aspirations places no limits on your ability. You are limited only by the thoughts you allow to occupy your mind. You can control whether those thoughts are empowering or discouraging. I allowed discouraging words to defer my dreams. But thankfully, I had encouragement from the people around me to persevere. Having positive influences in your life from family, friends, mother, father, aunt or uncle can enlarge your territory and help you create the breadth of vision that drives the proven values that underlie your convictions. Respect is a key proven value in this poem that gives permission to seize the authenticity of greatness.

My success in overcoming those discouraging episodes embodies the message of this poem. My aspirations could not rise to its potential because I allowed someone's negative words to minimize the positive words that were shared by many. My vision was broadened by an environment of love, support and encouragement. My conviction was solidified by the proven values that drives the passion for giving, nurturing and growing to all whom experience becoming dynamic.

Take a moment to reflect. You have had someone in your life who encouraged you. This person shared their heart with you because they wanted you to be successful. It could have been a teacher, principal, parent or another adult figure. You are at a point in your life where your fullest potential of success lies ahead. Reflect for a moment: did you heed their direction or did you ignore the direction? The true benefit of success come from not only the principles of this book, but from those who have walked the path you are about to embark upon. Experience is the best teacher. Listen, internalize, and execute those principles that have worked for others. My mother used to say, "If you just simply listen to my advice, it will prevent you from much of the heartbreak, hurt and heartache that your friends will encounter." I did listen. I did not do everything she said, but by acting on much of it provided outcomes that I can share now. The key to this is having someone pour into you the wisdom and the know-how to navigate the challenges of life. You subconsciously internalize words and actions that you may not use until the right situation presents itself. The bottom line is that the information is there, stored in your memory bank just waiting to be retrieved at the appropriate time.

Unfortunately, there are those who do not have this wisdom poured into their person. A scripture comes to mind: "Train up a child in the way he should go, and when he is old he will not depart from it" (Proverbs 22:6). He will return to the proven values that were placed inside. If these values were not placed inside, you have little or nothing to return to. You are in search of success that seems to escape you. If this wisdom was not poured into you earlier in life, it is not too late. It is being poured into you from my heart, body and soul as you read the words of this book. Reach out, grab the knowledge and soar to becoming dynamic.

We have experienced some of the growing pains, if you will, that you encounter and ultimately overcome as you experience the art of finessing the success factor. Now, we will expound upon tools that will help you leverage your dynamic strengths to garner the success you seek to achieve.

Dynamic People Advance Further

Dynamic people advance further because they are able to overcome fear and other limitations and move past their comfort zone. They identify what is hindering their success by utilizing the Before You Start questionnaire. In my experience, I find that it is our relationships with people in our lives that we allow to inhibit our success. It is lack of encouragement from people we respect and love. Let me make one fact clear: "Everyone that is good to you is not necessarily good for you." It is incumbent upon you to treat everyone with decency and respect; but that does not mean you should allow family members, friends and relatives who do not encourage you to a higher standard to have an influence in your life. People who discourage you have no place in your personal or professional space.

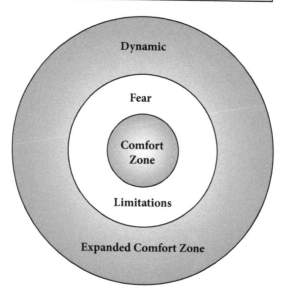

This illustration above shows how choosing to expand your comfort zone can help you on your journey to become dynamic. The center blue circle represents your existing or previous comfort zone. The white ring represents the limitations that keep you from personal and professional growth—fear, negative attitudes, and other limitations. The outer blue ring is your expanded comfort zone. When you break through these limitations in expanding your comfort zone, choose to include people in your life who empower you. Surround yourself with a circle of influence that focus on the reality of life's true value—happiness. Learn to tune out negativity. Increase your spiritual connection. Rely on your faith to expand your perception of the importance of humanity. Seek out individuals who can help you strengthen your walk in faith. When you break through barriers to becoming dynamic, you will experience success.

Most people are not happy with the choices they have made or the outcomes garnered in life and many times, their career. Every one of you reading this book has had people in your life who have encouraged you in a positive direction, but you refused to follow their counsel, even though they had your best interests at heart. If you reflect on the opportunities missed by not following those persons' advice, you can understand you have to make other choices in the future. My mantra is, "The choices you make can impact your life for the rest of your life." It is important to choose wisely. Don't blame others for your shortcomings. Don't simply talk about what needs to be done. Be about the business of making choices that drive positive results.

Failure to follow sound advice brings about choices that hinder success instead of driving it. Just because your choices have not garnered you the level of success you seek, it is not too late. You can choose the easy road or you can take the necessary steps on the front end and reap the benefits in the end stretch.

I once chose to allow discouraging words to defer my dream. Had I continued on the path of someone else's impression of my ability, I would not have grown to the person I am today. By following the advice of those who had my best interest at the center of their counsel, I was empowered by people in my corner to develop a plan to successfully navigate this temporary setback. The steps I took to turn this around was to first acknowledge that I allowed someone to determine the height of my aspirations. Then I focused on a mindset of excellence in all my pursuits. It included a plan of execution encompassing education, certifications, experience, community service and the ultimate honor, receiving an honorary doctorate in public service recognizing my public service. I was focused on "never again allowing anyone to stand in the way of my dreams." If you do not stand firm on what you believe, you will fall for that which does define your person.

Facing Up to Fear

Fear of the unknown is the reason most people have not reached their pinnacle of success. Fear can stand for "false evidence altering reality." Marianne Williamson (1992) places fear in this context in her poem, "Our Deepest Fear":

> Our deepest fear is not that we are inadequate.
> Our deepest fear is that we are powerful beyond measure.
> It is our light, not our darkness that most frightens us.
> We ask ourselves, Who am I to be brilliant, gorgeous,
>   talented, fabulous?
> Actually, who are you not to be? You are a child of God.
> Your playing small does not serve the world.
> There is nothing enlightened about shrinking so that other
>   people won't feel insecure around you.
> We are all meant to shine, as children do.
> We were born to make manifest the glory of God that is
>   within us.
> It's not just in some of us; it's in everyone.
> And as we let our own light shine, we unconsciously give
>   other people permission to do the same.
> As we are liberated from our own fear, our presence
>   automatically liberates others.

A savvy businesswoman who has been instrumental in my life started her business in 1982 amid discouragement, sparse funding and a prohibitive environment for women-owned businesses. Listening to those who told her that she would not make it, caused her great apprehension. She was told the time was not right. She felt great fear and anxiety. Because she drew from her faith and believed that she was more than a conqueror, however, she remained true to her goals and overcame the words of discouragement.

She took a leap of faith, saved her money, enrolled in trade school and completed the courses and practical training to become a cosmetologist. She is highly successful with a client base that attests to the fact that she is the best at her craft. She weathered the storms that face a small business and emerged as a savvy businesswoman who undeniably carries the torch of success, lighting the path for others to follow. She is a woman of faith who continues my mother and father's legacy of humility and service to humanity. The woman that I reference is my sister, my hero, the guiding light in my life.

My sister overcame fear by identifying its origin and internalizing the message, "Fear will not control my destiny." In my case, because someone discouraged me, I internalized the fear factor and doubted that I possessed power beyond measure to conquer fear. I had reached a crossroads. Now, as I write this book, for the first time in my life, fear has been placed in the archives of historical reference. When fear of success is doused by confronting the limitations that beset you, the dynamic persona can surface and you have achieved the victory and becoming dynamic awaits you.

In expanding your comfort zone, limitations become minimized and your focus on success becomes maximized. As you follow this path, success can be realized and that dynamic individual can emerge with confidence and self-assuredness. As confidence and self-assuredness prevail, success in your endeavors becomes evident.

Creating Opportunities That Sustain Your Success

Years after my first wardrobe consultation at my friend's house, I was appointed by the international president of Sigma Gamma Rho Sorority, Inc. to serve on its international board responsible for developing and maintaining youth affiliate programs. The purpose of the organization is to promote and strengthen the economic, social and civic viability of our communities. At regional conferences devoted to these goals, undergraduate student members with ambition and aspirations to advance to higher positions would ask me, "How did you get appointed to the international board?" Several factors came into play, as I will explain after this story.

Not long before I was appointed to the International Board of Sigma Gamma Rho Sorority, Inc. in 2010, I planned the largest youth symposium in the Denver metro area in 2009. I had no idea of the impact this would have. The focus of the program was to expose youth to successful business owners and medical professionals. Over two hundred young people attended. With my connections in the area and my community service, I singlehandedly raised over $4,000 to fund the project, by contacting people in my circle of influence.

The most challenging goal was to sell the concept to the decision maker, the principal of the high school where the symposium was to be held. This was not an easy task, but my image and commitment to excellence sold the principal on the idea. After the principal was on board, he gave me permission to present the idea to the PTA to garner support from parents. The symposium was a huge success, and the youth left with a renewed sense of confidence, equipped with the tools to make life-changing decisions and to enhance their success in life and career.

Early in 2010, I attended a reception after a National Pan-Hellenic conference where I was introduced to the leadership of Sigma Gamma Rho sorority, of which I was a member. Our discussion centered on the sorority's mission of empowering youth. I utilized this opportunity to communicate my heartfelt commitment to our mission by describing the youth symposium I coordinated and the lives it touched in a positive way. My goal was not to be appointed to the international board, but communicating this success story to the international president created an opportunity.

In Sigma Gamma Rho's ninety years of existence, I was the first from the Denver area to be appointed to the position of overseeing international youth affiliate programs. During my tenure, international youth enrollment increased 58 percent from July 2010 to July 2014 (from 500 to 788 youth members). The increase was due to creating a consistent marketing strategy and streamlining operations.

When the undergraduate members at regional conferences asked me, "What are the drivers for your success?" I outlined three compelling strategies that were instrumental in finessing my success. First, have no fear or hesitation in communicating your success to people who are in a decision-making capacity. The opportunity presented itself and I was ready to communicate my success. Second, if you want to be in a position of power or influence, you must be in the environment with people who have position and power and who can impact your success. The conference presented a networking opportunity to leverage my experience. Third, you must communicate your methods of execution and the result garnered.

So, fourteen years after I allowed a negative person to delay my dream of becoming an image consultant, I was able to use my leadership skills to help youth achieve their dreams at the local and national scale. In 2005, I started my own nonprofit, Dynamic Images by the Hairston Group®, professional style at its finest. My consulting business, Dynamic Images International LLC, evolved from my twenty-five year career in corporate America, which has given me the skills to help up-and-coming professionals and future executives succeed in the business world.

Create Your Own Success

There are several key strategies to creating your own opportunity for success. Identifying key players and a knowledge of your business is essential for creating opportunity for yourself. In your workplace, opportunity can take the form of developing a means of smoother department operations, more efficient workflow, and cost-saving measures. Creating opportunity through serving your community can help you develop skills that lead to advancement in the company or can add a significant achievement to the community-service component of your résumé.

Dynamic people are visionaries who step up to the plate to seize the opportunity to forge their success. It is one thing to have a vision, but the visionary can execute the vision and bring the thought or concept behind it to fruition. Whether it is planning your approach to serve on a national board or planning your strategy as you embark upon new horizons, it is mission-critical that you understand the importance of finessing the success factor to be used to your fullest potential in becoming dynamic.

Having acted on your indwelling desire to be successful, identify your passion and move forward to attain it. Understanding your purpose is important. Your purpose thrives on the passion that gives meaning to your goals. The keys to a sense of purpose are developed in chapter 6.

There are a number of academics who use quantitative methods to minimize or even refute the role purpose plays in understanding your life's work. I do not argue with their research. I share the principles that drive my success. Purpose and passion are the ingredients for becoming dynamic.

As you begin to realize your own success, a greater sense of self-esteem emerges and gives you a renewed level of confidence in your ability. You are responsible for reaching out for assistance in your quest. Much of what has preceded gives you what you need for fueling your success. It takes having people in your corner to make your success a reality. In his book *Success Runs in our Race*, George Fraser states, "It used to be about who you know, now it is about what who you know knows about you."

My plan for finessing success provides direction to all whose desire is to overcome fear, break through limitations, create opportunities, and achieve the pinnacle of success in all they endeavor. It has worked for many. I am confident it could make a difference for you.

———————

Over twenty-five years, as my career expanded, I was consistently defined by my clients as "driven." The determination, tenacity, and drive to succeed sustained me throughout my career. My success was substantiated by my ability to consistently perform at a level that garnered significant recognition for outstanding performance. Sometimes, when there were moments that I questioned my purpose, I would take a moment to reflect on the many plaques, trophies and mementos that are displayed in my office. For the many opportunities to leverage my ability that opened doors and gave me the confidence to share this book with you, I am truly grateful.

6

Career Advancement

Preparation Creates Dynamic Opportunities

CAREER ADVANCEMENT IS THE sixth compelling strategy for success. You advance your career when you incorporate activities that support your quest for upward mobility. These are activities that develop your talents, optimize your potential, increase your employability, and help you realize your dreams and aspirations. The work you have done to this point in the book sets the foundation for your career advancement.

This chapter is dedicated to those who want to move from the ordinary to the extraordinary. It provides tools that will help you reach the pinnacle of your success, find total satisfaction in what you do for your life's work, and enhance your worth to your employer. In this process, always ask, "How do I make them want more of me?" It is mission-critical that you understand how to position yourself for opportunity.

Enhance Your Self-Worth

The Relative Success Pyramid is a tool for assessing your level of career achievement; it places responsibility for success in your hands. It is up to you to determine where you want to be in the pyramid. Dynamic people are consistently among the high achievers in the 3 percent gradient. They are deeply respected. They thrive on empowering others within their circle of influence. They are willing to incorporate proven values in all aspects of life. The 10 percent gradient represents those who have not reached their fullest potential and therefore still striving for success. The 67 percent gradient represents individuals who have not grasped the concept of becoming dynamic. They accept average and the bare minimum of achievement. The 20 percent gradient represents those who are unemployed. They are seeking the benefit that becoming dynamic can provide to jumpstart their career. They enter the workplace armed with the tools to reach the pinnacle of their success. If you desire to move from the 67 percent or 20 percent gradients to the 3 percent, you can do so by following the principles outlined in this chapter. Our focus is on the ultimate, not the mundane—excellence without excuses—and responsibility without compromise.

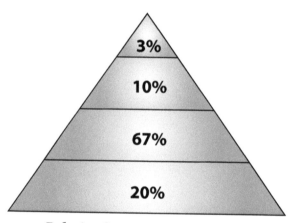

Relative Success Pyramid (RSP)

The Relative Success Pyramid not only provides a method of assessing where you are in your career advancement cycle, it will motivate you to incorporate the compelling strategies needed to get you to the place you would like to be. For example at the 10 percent gradient you may determine you need to identify a mentor and a sponsor. At 67 percent, you may need more education in your field of expertise. You have been provided much of what you need to move to the pinnacle of your success.

Another powerful tool to be utilized in the career advancement space is the Core Process Continuum, which illustrates the components that support career advancement. The Core Process Continuum is comprised of three components: (a) career preparation, (b) career opportunity and (c) career success.

Core Process

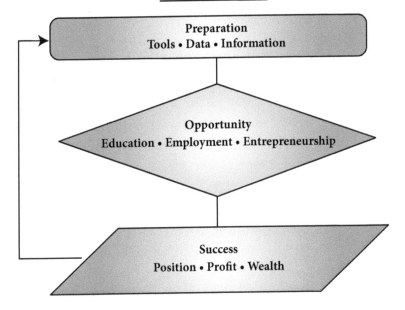

The Core Process Continuum is a critical process for career advancement that demonstrates how preparation plus opportunity equals success. Use the Core Process Worksheet on page 113 to keep track of how you are utilizing preparation and opportunity to move toward success. This dynamic combination is at the core of career development.

Preparation

The core process begins with career preparation, whereby you utilize available tools, data and information that enhance your career advancement. Many of the tools for career preparation have been discussed—your image, your brand, building relationships, excellence, professional presentation and verbal and non-verbal communication. Now you must equip yourself with the tangible assets that will propel you to higher levels of success and ultimately to the position you seek.

Résumé

Your résumé must be clear, concise and to the point. It introduces you in your absence. The résumé should contain power words that bring you and the experience you are communicating to life. Begin with a highly focused employment objective conveying your commitment to the company, while keeping your career growth and development front and center.

Far too many times, I have observed résumés that are "me-centric." Your objective should be mutually beneficial to you and the company. Remember: the company is asking, "What's in it for me?" You may want to tailor your objective to a company you are applying to, but having the basics will allow you to revise your objective easily.

Choose an approach for organizing your work experiences, either *chronological* or *functional* (there are many resources on the Internet for guidance on the best approach). Once you have your experiences on paper, get a mentor or knowledgeable friend or colleague to review your résumé. Have multiple people proofread it so it is perfect. Selection of paper is another important consideration. Use "watermarked" résumé — grade neutral color paper — white, buff or soft blue. Avoid photos on your résumé.

Core Process Worksheet

Here you can keep track of your tangible assets and achievements. Use this worksheet as a motivational tool that encourages you to review your assets and write down opportunities you will explore to advance your career.

Preparation: Collect Your Tangible Assets ☐ Résumé ☐ Social media presence ☐ Brag book ☐ Members of your support network Opportunity: Expand Your Value ☐ Educational opportunities ☐ Professional associations ☐ Networking ☐ Job boards ☐ Mentors and sponsors	To-do list: _____ _____ _____ _____ _____ _____ _____ _____ _____ _____ _____ _____

Social Media Presence

LinkedIn and other professional social media outlets are good ways to maintain a professional presence in the business world. Be sure your online biography is as carefully worded and up to date as your résumé. Invest in a professional photograph to enhance your online image.

Brag Book

Develop a "brag book." This is a compilation of all your awards, certificates and recognitions. If you are mentioned in a magazine or newspaper, include a copy of the article. Keeping this organized and in a readily accessible place will prove to be a valuable resource in your career advancement plan.

Opportunity

Career opportunity is created because you have invested the time in education and training. Education is a powerful tool that, once you have it, no one can take away. If you are struggling against the glass ceiling that seems impenetrable for many, investing in education can give you the skills that will make you stand apart. By expanding your educational horizons, you will be prepared to seize the opportunities that present themselves and project the image that you have the desire to succeed.

Internal company-wide management development programs provide a pathway to advancement. This type of program prepares you for greater responsibility, as you build an understanding of the career path you seek. You should inquire about the opportunity for training and development soon after you begin work at a new company. Internal training opportunities can move you from one level to the next and beyond and may bring you together with people who are in a position to advance your career. Never miss an opportunity to share your accomplishments with them. Following internal job postings is essential to stay connected with career opportunities that exist within the company. Internal networking can take many forms in the way of keeping abreast of the data available to you to advance your career. Your mentor and/or sponsor is key in this process.

If your company uses a management assessment tool, take advantage of it. These assessments are designed to drive behavior change that leads to more successful outcomes when managing people, policy and projects.

Opportunities for building skills and expanding your horizons exist through on-line degrees, adult education classes, and certification programs. Certification adds validity to your skill and powers the level of expertise it takes to support your ultimate business goals. For example, I taught etiquette successfully for many years, using my own experiences growing up and my own research. I ultimately invested in certification as a corporate etiquette consultant in order to increase my level of professional recognition, which complemented my existing expertise.

Many Chambers of Commerce provide career advancement programs that prepare up-and-coming and future executives for management-level positions.

You may also attend conferences and workshops as resources for adding to your knowledge base and creating professional networks. Memberships in professional organizations in your area of career focus is essential for staying abreast of career opportunities and current educational certificates.

There is an abundance of information in social media that can advance your career and create a circle of colleagues from whom you can acquire career leads.

As you build your skills and advance your career, preparing for an interview is among the most important information-gathering opportunities you will have. Whether interviewing for a position internally or externally, gather as much information about the person interviewing you (internally) or the company (externally). This information gathering process helps you develop intelligent questions. You may know the answer to the question you are asking; but you are asking the question to let the interviewer know just how much you know about the company. The inquisitive you will reveal itself. The amount of research you choose to invest will differentiate you from the other candidates.

Success in the career advancement space is achieved when, through your hard work and focus, you arrive on the career path of your dreams. Once you are in your chosen career, you must exercise the same proven values that it took to land the job. As you work hard, remain steadfast in your pursuit, becoming dynamic is imminent.

One outcome of your success is often higher profits for the company; your personal wealth will also benefit as a result.

Financial Literacy

Creating wealth is a topic unto itself. Your advancement in position and salary is driven by your economic benefit to the company, whether your job is in sales, accounting, communications, or any other area. However, the income you acquire (whatever the career) can only be sustained by investing and wise money management.

Understanding the importance and responsibility that goes along with credit is of critical importance, especially if you are in an industry where your credit score is assessed as part of the interview and hiring process. Personal finance and business practices are often intertwined, and the sense of financial well-being from having stable finances contributes to your ability to be a dynamic presence in the workplace.

The Value of Networking

The art of networking is a valuable tool that can open up major opportunities in your career advancement process. We covered internal networking earlier. However, you must proceed strategically with a plan in mind.

I happen to believe that the people you meet, you do so for a very specific purpose. Meeting people could be for a reason, a season or a lifetime. But most people occupy a larger purpose than is initially perceived. The purpose most frequently is not revealed immediately, but in time it will. This brings to mind a scripture in John 13:7, "You do not realize now what I am doing, but later you will understand." A spiritual that my mother used to sing to me as a child embellishes this thought quite well: "We will understand it better by and by."

As you network and build alliances, you will want to take note of my Networking Basics plan on pages 117-118. Use it to help you refine your networking approach.

Networking Basics

Make a Strong Entrance

- Think strategically about why you are there, and pursue your goal deliberately
- Be mindful of your manners, posture, eye contact
- To enter a group, make eye contact with a listener or the speaker
- Look for a happy face and focus there first
- When entering a room, it is your responsibility to make the first move—you are there to network
- Leave a lasting impression through your dress and deportment (your brand)

Put Your People Skills to Work

- ❖ Listen Attentively
  - Focus on the speaker
  - Watch for clues, feelings conveyed through body language
  - Identify areas of mutual interest
  - Keep an open mind

- ❖ Personify Self-Confidence
  - Initiate conversations
  - Like yourself enough to share yourself with others
  - Your self-assurance assures others
  - Self-confidence allows you to be assertive without being aggressive
  - Be eager to share opinions and exchange ideas

- ❖ Communicate Effectively
  - Use verbal/nonverbal communication
  - Adopt voice inflection
  - Paraphrase for clarity to show your interest
  - Respond from the listener's reality

- ❖ Be Willing to Share
  - Empowering others will encourage them to help you
  - Show fundamental respect for people
  - Listen with an open mind
  - The more value you communicate, the more others will feel drawn to you

❖ Be Inquisitive
- Ask intelligent questions
- Build upon information others share
- Introduce new ideas and perspectives
- Value the knowledge of others
- Clarify your needs to the individual
- Ask open-ended questions (beginning with who, what, when, where and why)

Know Introduction Etiquette

- When introducing men and women to each other, rank prevails over gender
- When introducing a customer to business associates, treat the customer as superior to honor the relationship— say the customer's name first
- When introducing a superior to a subordinate, use the superior's name first
- When introducing peers to each other, use either name first
- When introducing older people to younger people, use the older person's name first
- When introducing persons with no business status, age prevails to show honor
- When introducing persons of status (Senator, Congressman, Pastor), status prevails and their name is used first

Make a Graceful Exit from a Conversation

- Excuse yourself tactfully
- Show appreciation for the time shared
- Set a specific time to meet if you want to continue networking
- Shake hands and exchange cards
- Be selective about to whom you give a business card

Networking opportunities occur in a variety of contexts: business networking socials; art galleries; political events; professional organizations; fraternity, sorority and alumnae events; in the mentor/coach/sponsor relationship; and social networks. Unplanned encounters are networking opportunities, too.

If food is being served at the networking event, your goal is not to pile your plate with food and attempt to work the room. You are there to meet people, not to eat. If you think you will be hungry, eat before you come to the event. That said, the place where food is displayed is the center of attention. It makes a great place to position yourself to network—but not with your mouth full.

Give Yourself a Promotion—Start Your Own Business

Networking is especially critical if you are thinking about starting your own business. Your corporate career has provided you with many useful skills. Give yourself a promotion by starting your own company. The expertise and experience that you have gained in your present position could prove beneficial in your quest to fulfill your career goals. Whether you are working for a corporation or become an entrepreneur, you must develop a plan that will sustain you whether you advance your career at your current organization or if you choose to start your own company.

Career opportunity, whether networking, starting your own business, pursuing educational opportunities, or finding a supportive mentor, is the key to using the Core Process to your advantage. A prime example of creating opportunity was the youth symposium I referenced earlier. Years of etiquette workshop facilitation and community service, together with the model of that symposium, now form the basis of Dynamic Images by the Hairston Group®.

Dynamic Images International LLC is a culmination of my professional experience and lifelong commitment to effectively impact the life and career of others. My website, www.dynamicimages4you.com, connects the two enterprises.

Clarify Your Sense of Purpose

Earlier in the chapter, we talked about assessing and compiling your tangible assets. As you plan for career advancement, it helps to keep some intangible assets in mind as well. Your sense of purpose is foremost among these intangibles. As I discuss in chapter 3, substance is a critical quality of leaders. As you reflect on your career path, I developed the exercise on page 121 to help you and others reflect on your sense of purpose, the passion that underlies your substance, the legacy of your actions, and how these things come together in your journey to becoming dynamic.

Upon completion of this process, you will discover still another set of tools to clarify in your mind the direction of your path to success and in becoming dynamic. Now as you attend networking events, you can seize the opportunity that awaits you in building and understanding the impact you make in the image you present. Your presence in motion is established. You are equipped with the tools to incorporate power words and proven values in your introductions. The diamond in the rough is now radiating with clarity, depth and definition. You have arrived, the pinnacle of your success is near; reach out and grasp the information. The success you have created for the future is near. Career advancement is imminent. Becoming dynamic, your primary objective is achieved.

A Sense of Purpose

What Is Your Purpose? ➤ Valuable business asset ➤ Essential for career growth ➤ Take risks ➤ Making tough decisions ➤ Create new opportunities that enrich personal and professional destiny	_____ _____ _____ _____ _____
Essence of Your Mission Statement ➤ Outline your passion ➤ Things which are most passionate about ➤ Tied to having a positive impact on people ➤ Your proficiencies ➤ Things that you do extremely well ➤ Things you have learned over time ➤ Things that friends and family have complimented you on	_____ _____ _____ _____ _____ _____ _____
Your Purpose, Defined ➤ Your Reason ➤ Your Function or Intention ➤ Give meaning or shape to your goals ➤ Keep you focused ➤ Make you passionate	_____ _____ _____ _____ _____
Determine Your Legacy ➤ What you desire to do in life can define your persona ➤ The impact you want to have on the world/marketplace ➤ The way you want to be remembered ➤ Manifest your purpose with confidence, clarity, satisfaction	_____ _____ _____ _____ _____

7

Community Service

Becoming Dynamic by Giving Back

G IVING BACK TO YOUR community is the seventh compelling
strategy for success. Community service is the external outlet
that not only fulfills your desire to serve, it builds networks and
strengthens your brand. Corporations want their employees to serve
their communities. This not only fulfills the commitment to community, which is the goal of most corporations, it provides visibility and
strengthens the brand of the corporation as well. A distinction should
be made between volunteering and community service. Community
service is sometimes performed to fulfill a requirement, but for the
purposes of this chapter, we will focus on community service from
the perspective of volunteerism. Whether intended or unintended,
community service can be a means of self-actualization. Your desire
to succeed can be achieved through community service.

My very first award, which is appropriately mounted on the wall
in my office, came as a result of my service to the community through
the United Way. I served on the Board of Mile High Child Care
Association, a United Way agency, for several years. I received the
award of Board Member of the year. More importantly, my employer,
allowed me to serve as a "Loaned Executive" to United Way for the
entire campaign season. The experience was most valuable and
gave me exposure to many types of businesses. The career opportunities and mentor relationships afforded by the level of exposure
in this capacity provided career advancement opportunities and

the opportunity to meet individuals who had a profound impact on my life and career.

Community Service Builds Networks

As many of you have reviewed my biography, you have seen the level of community service in which I engaged over the years (www.dynamicimagesintl.com). It was a desire that came naturally, because I grew up in an environment where my parents inherently served the community.

My mother served in many positions in the church. She served as confidant and guidance counselor to ministers. She was the poll watcher and precinct captain for our community. She attended meetings about community issues, with me as a little girl in tow, with my notepad and pencil in hand. My job was to communicate to her, from my perspective, the details of the meeting. I was always on task because I knew there would be a surprise after I made my report. My mother initiated many gestures of kindness. If someone was out of work due to sickness or loss of a job, she made sure that food was collected from the community for the family. If someone passed away, she would make sure money was collected for a community wreath. She had a home daycare center for children. Children learned how to read and developed social skills by the time they started first grade. Our home was on a corner where the bus picked up the children in our community for school. My mother made sure all kids at the bus stop had breakfast before going to school. She served as the bus monitor. She served lunch in the school cafeteria. She was an active participant in and an advocate at PTA meetings. Our home was where people were welcomed for breakfast, lunch and dinner and where church members came to eat dinner after church. My father was supportive of my mother's efforts. She never had to ask permission to do all she did. My dad was always on board and was serving beside her.

I have shared stories about my mother and father with you in order to give you a sense of the values they instilled in me and the role community service plays in becoming dynamic. It is noteworthy to focus on community service as one of the strategies for success because you can fulfill the need to achieve through community service when your professional life in corporate America is not meeting that need.

My twenty-five year career garnered many successes, four-time President's Club winner and multiple region and district sales awards; however, there were moments when I felt insecure about my path. In my career, recognition and achieving sales results was a driving factor for accessing ability and success. You can be in the top ranks one year and not the next. Community service grounded me in my pursuit for success at times when I was not fully achieving my goals. In times like these, community service work kept me motivated to achieve the next level. Serving my community gave me a sense of fulfillment in those down times. My focus on others helped me reach my ultimate self-actualization.

I did not serve the community for recognitions or awards; however, recognition and awards were the net result of my community service. When you are serving from the heart with the intent to purely serve your community, your sincerity prevails, people notice and thus recognition occurs. Community service can place you in a position where you become a power broker in your community. You become a resource. You evolve into the person the community calls on for your expertise. In establishing your brand in your community in this way, reciprocation is a pleasure, not an inconvenience.

Community Service Is a Catalyst for Position and Power

Despite all your efforts, from time to time you might have a manager who decides, for whatever reason, you will go no further in your career. You are at the top of your salary range, you have executed many of the strategies I have covered, and still you find yourself at a crossroads. You love your job, but you must make a decision. Community service to the rescue. Community service can help fill the void while you plan your strategy for success in your current position. Community service may even help to plan your exodus to greener pastures. Here again, you may use the skills you acquire from community service as the springboard for starting your own business.

At times like these, serve your community, and your self-esteem will get a boost. It is during these times that you need encouragement and a cause. It is community service that can provide the motivation you need.

In community service, your commitment, your character and your cause are paramount. Typically the organization is counting on you to follow through with your time commitment. Your character in your community substantiates what you bring to the organization. Your passion for the cause will determine your commitment and contribution, and you will be recognized for your dedication.

Community service can help you gain experience and confidence in your career objective. Community service changes lives. It is an opportunity for you to share positive experiences with others that you would not otherwise have the opportunity to do.

Fundraising as a Power Tool

An integral part of service to your community is your ability to raise funds to support the program you are passionate about. You are leveraging your power and influence as you embark upon motivating stakeholders—potential donors—to support your cause.

My strategy to bring this process to fruition is fundraising from a community-based approach. You may seek out grants that are focused on your particular cause. Lastly, you may approach this from a grassroots perspective—roll up your sleeves, plan your approach, use your service to your community as your major motivator and get on with the business of serving others.

Private funds are available in your community to support your projects. You just have to identify stakeholders who share your passion for a specific cause. When raising funds for the youth symposium referenced earlier, I identified stakeholders with whom I served on community projects, social organizations and political forums, all having similar causes at the center of our efforts.

Before I go further, everything you have learned from the preceding chapters—your dynamic presence, your brand, your proven values, your relationship skills, your ability to finesse success despite adversity, and your plan for career advancement—should be in place before you embark upon fundraising. Becoming dynamic is key as you position yourself to garner support for your cause.

First, you must identify potential stakeholders. Stakeholders are individuals who have supported you in the past and who are passionate about the cause you promote. Stakeholders can be found at social events, political networking events, social clubs and organizations, conferences and at any place where people congregate. Stakeholders enhance your circle of influence, not only for funding your project, but strengthening your brand among people you want to include in your circle of influence in becoming dynamic. Your approach should be to strike up a conversation to seek out common interests. Identify the interests of your potential stakeholder. You gain buy-in from your community by being visible in your community. This means not just being present at events, but becoming a dynamic and integral part of the environment at the event. "You must learn how to effectively work the room."

You should consider everyone you meet as a potential stakeholder, ruling no one out unless you determine that there is simply no interest in your cause. Your mission, your messaging and your value proposition statement should be clearly communicated in order for the person to be able to clearly identify if your cause parallels their own. Clearly communicate what you need and why it is needed. Before you make "the ask," trial-close your potential donor with questions confirming clarity on what you communicated. And, finally close on a timeframe based on the timing of the company budget. Select your words carefully. Always smile, be gracious and exercise the utmost in professionalism. Remember: the stakeholder buys into your credibility, integrity and business acumen. Then, and only then will your cause occupy a place of importance in the mind of your stakeholder.

Don't be afraid to make "the ask." Potential stakeholders have a right to say no. Just remember: "The no's you get move you closer to a yes." Passion and perseverance have caused many a donor follow up a "no" with a "yes."

Before you embark on the process of fundraising, do your research, plan your strategy and work your plan. Refer to the networking plan and sense of purpose in chapter 6. My approach in working my plan was centered on submitting a letter to my potential stakeholders that outlined my program. This worked for me because I had a business or community service relationship with many potential stakeholders. I followed up in person and by telephone to make the ask and close the deal.

You can support your fundraising efforts and get tax benefits for your donors in a variety of ways. You can find a fiscal sponsor, such as a nonprofit agency that shares your goals, which will submit grant applications on your behalf. Community foundations can set up an account for your cause that will accept donations and offer a tax benefit for donors. You may use crowdsourcing through Indiegogo, Go Fund Me, or other sites as a way to raise funds, as well. The ultimate step is to establish your own 501(c)(3) nonprofit corporation.

Service to your community is an integral component in becoming dynamic. The business world is known as cutthroat, focused only on money. That doesn't mean that you have to let that mindset control your life and your values. Giving back to your community does good, it enriches your life, and it positions you as a person of substance and character that is sure to be recognized.

Conclusion

THE CONTENT AND SUBSTANCE of my personal journey with you have been experienced in the "7 Compelling Strategies for Success" presented here. Your destiny is closer than you imagine. By reading *Becoming Dynamic*, you have taken the first step in optimizing your potential. *Becoming Dynamic* allowed you to uncover your authenticity of greatness. Your authenticity of greatness is realized because you have taken the time to invest in the added value that the seven strategies contribute to the pinnacle of your success. As you move forward, you now have a plan that drives powerful introductions, containing power words and proven values that forge strong business relationships. Now you understand that the impact you make in the image that you present can, in fact, determine your success. Your presence in motion is revealed in your confidence in every action. "No man or woman is an island unto themselves." The relationships you build when developing a mentor and sponsor substantiate your readiness to embark on more responsibility and upward mobility in your career. The drive, determination and tenacity to succeed have become a reality, as you govern your actions by the guiding principles acquired for your professional portfolio.

You are armed with the tools that embody excellence as you remain true to your dynamic standard. Excellence starts with you. The proven values conveyed in *Becoming Dynamic* prepare you for realizing the excellence you possess. Because you do not know where opportunity will present itself, your actions are the point of reference that others use to make an informed decision on your behalf and in your favor. Your demeanor, your image and your brand speak volumes about who you are and the standard you represent. Opportunity can be found in almost any environment. It is your responsibility to be ready to seize the moment. *Becoming Dynamic* provides the strategies to make this a reality.

We have all heard the old adage that some people are simply born to be leaders, and rightfully so. This is a statement that I will not refute. However, *Becoming Dynamic* takes a different approach. It directs your path to leadership by guiding you through strategies that place the responsibility on you to internalize the substance, savvy and style that motivate others to follow. It is centered in the perspective that you are born with the talent, and it helps you understand your potential and define your persona as a leader. You have the tools for greatness, but if you do not have a sound plan and results-oriented approach, there will be a gap between your desires and the impact you make before your time on earth has expired. *Becoming Dynamic* is the bridge that connects the two. Its strategies add the dimensions that allow you to have more, be more and do more in your life and career. Let's not be complacent. Be proactive and become the dynamic person you are intended to be.

Seeking higher levels of success and ultimately career advancement is the goal of becoming dynamic. Satisfaction in life, in yourself and in your accomplishments is a central theme. The words and experiences to help you achieve this are in this book, but it is only through *your* actions that your potential can be realized. I challenge you to try the strategies in *Becoming Dynamic*. My life, passion and dedication have been poured into this work for you. It is my intent that as you read and implement Becoming Dynamic, your destiny can be achieved and joy attained.

There are no guarantees in life or in this book, for that matter, but *Becoming Dynamic* provides an awareness that there is more to be, to do, to have and achieve in your quest for success and ultimately, becoming dynamic.

Thank you for taking this journey through *Becoming Dynamic* with me, and please share it with your community, friends, business colleagues and all who will embrace it as a guide to reaching the pinnacle of success in life and career.

Works of Interest

Deliberate and strategic thought has been given in the selection of these works of interest that follow; they complement my work over the last sixteen years in developing the strategies for *Becoming Dynamic*. I share these works of interest with you in the hope that they will be useful as you embark upon a new chapter in your life.

Etiquette and Manners

American School of Protocol, Atlanta, Georgia. www.theamericanschoolofprotocol.com.

Johnson, Dorothea, and Denise Hilton-Campbell. 1997. *The Little Book of Etiquette*. Philadelphia, PA: Running Press.

Li, Bing-nan. 1991. *Daily Manners: The Essentials of Courtesy*. http://online.sfsu.edu/rone/China/manners.htm.

Success in the Corporate World

Fast, Julius. 1970. *Body Language*. New York: M. Evans.

Iscoe, Stephan. 1998. "12-Step Plan for Personal Success." www.4hb.com/08twelvepointpersonals.html.

Works Cited in the Text

Hughes, Langston. 1951. "Harlem." *Montage of a Dream Deferred*. New York: Henry Holt.

Etiquepedia. 2014. "Ptah-Hotep's Early Egyptian Teachings on Etiquette." 27 February 2014. http://etiquipedia.blogspot.com/2014/02/ptah-hoteps-early-egyptian-teachings-on.html.

The Holy Bible: Old and New Testaments in the King James Version. 1970. Camden, NJ: T. Nelson.

Fraser, George C. 1994. *Success Runs in Our Race: The Complete Guide to Effective Networking in the African-American Community.* New York: William Morrow.

Wiencek, Henry. 1999. *The Hairstons: An American Family in Black and White.* New York: St. Martin's Press.

Williamson, Marianne. 1992. "Our Deepest Fear,." *A Return To Love: Reflections on the Principles of a Course in Miracles.* New York: Harper Collins.

About the Author

Elma Hairston's mantra is helping individuals become dynamic. She focuses on creating unique programs and tools that help her clients, partners and many others become dynamic by developing talent, optimizing potential, building human capital, increasing employability, enhancing quality of life and contributing to the realization of dreams and aspirations.

Elma is a national presenter known for her thought-provoking and highly interactive sessions, which have led to substantial change in the lives of youth, up-and-coming professionals, and future executives. A highly talented expert in the human capital arena, Elma is currently the president of Dynamic Images by the Hairston Group®, a nonprofit focused on career development for youth. She is also founder and managing director of Dynamic Images International LLC, through which she advises executives and up-and-coming professionals on maximizing their career potential. Elma is the first to introduce the concept of Dynamic Image Career Advancement Consultant, which she defines as a dynamic person highly skilled at personal development who is compensated for making career and image recommendations.

In her role as Dynamic Image Career Advancement Consultant, Elma challenges clients to embrace change and focus on professional progress. Elma firmly believes that professional progress hinges on one's ability to effectively manage constant change in life and business.

Elma Hairston began her career in banking with First Interstate Bank (now Wells Fargo), and was a senior executive sales professional with Johnson & Johnson for over twenty-five years. She has been actively involved in community affairs for over thirty years. She launched her nonprofit, Dynamic Images by the Hairston Group®, in 2005, and Dynamic Images International LLC in 2015 to share her experience in the corporate world with others. Elma has spoken to business audiences and youth nationwide, and was appointed to the national Board of Sigma Gamma Rho Sorority, Inc.

Elma is a recipient of the following awards: Random Acts of Kindness Award (Sister's Foundation); African Americans Who Make A Difference Award (Denver Urban Spectrum Newspaper); Achievements in Business Award (Colorado Black Women for Political Action); Citizen of the Year Award (Kappa Alpha Psi Fraternity); Heart of Humility Award (Colorado Sisterhood Crusade); and Salute to Black Women Award (National Council of Negro Women). In addition to the awards, she received a letter of commendation for mentoring girls from the Lieutenant Governor (State of Colorado). Elma chaired the marketing committee for the Boy Scouts of America and served on the Board of Mile High Child Care Association (a United Way Agency); the Board of the League of Women Voters; the Martin Luther King Humanitarian Awards Committee; and Board of Health and Human Services of Guilford County, North Carolina.

She has been selected as a panel participant in political candidate forums. Elma is a former president of Colorado Black Women for Political Action; Women's and Youth Department (King Baptist Church); and the Graduate Chapter of Beta Rho Sigma, Denver Alumnae Chapter (2008–2012). She has written several articles for a community newspaper and developed and facilitated youth programs. Born in High Point, North Carolina, Elma received a degree in business from Regis University, a Jesuit university located in Denver, Colorado. Elma is also the recipient of an Honorary Doctorate in Public Service.

To learn more about Elma Hairston,
visit www.dynamicimagesintl.com.

To learn more about her conferences, workshops
and how to order copies of *Becoming Dynamic*,
visit www.dynamicimages4you.com.

CPSIA information can be obtained
at www.ICGtesting.com
Printed in the USA
JSHW050511080222
22696JS00004B/26